MW01001815

THE CHURCH OF LIVING DANGEROUSLY

TALES OF A DRUG-RUNNING MEGACHURCH PASTOR

JOHN LEE BISHOP

HARPER HORIZON

The Church of Living Dangerously

Published by Harper Horizon, an imprint of HarperCollins Focus LLC.

ISBN 978-1-4002-5159-9 (HC)
ISBN 978-1-4002-5161-2 (ePub)

Library of Congress Control Number: 2024949567

Printed in the United States of America

24 25 26 27 28 LBC 5 4 3 2 1

To Michelle
My wife, my best friend, the mother of our three amazing children, and the best grandma to our eight grandkids.

Contents

Part 3: Papa John

Part 4: 65782–298

Part 5: Almost Home

Prologue

This is the last time.

Around five o'clock in the morning on December 11, 2017, I drove north on the highway. To my right the sun was just beginning to peek out over the low foothills of Mexico. Up ahead and slightly to the left, I could see the blue lights of the border checkpoint blinking weakly against the dark sky.

All I have to do is get across, I thought. *Then I'll be done.*

Done with drug running. Done with the cartel. Done with always looking over my shoulder for men with guns.

I gripped the steering wheel and felt the sweat from my palms.

Outside, the temperature hovered around fifty degrees. But the interior of the car was hotter than hell.

Under normal circumstances I'd have cranked the air-conditioning and eased the seat back, maybe thrown on a local rock radio station to calm me down.

But I couldn't do that.

The car's AC unit was gone. So was the stereo system. In their place was a large quantity of marijuana, freshly grown in the fields of Nayarit, Mexico. About three days earlier, the car had been gutted, then filled to the brim with product by some guys from the Sinaloa Cartel. Now it was a roving dispensary. There was weed in the front bumper, weed in the back bumper, and weed secured to the bottom of the car with duct tape.

If I'd hit the eject button on my CD player, it probably would have spit out a joint.

Moving slowly up the road at a few miles over the speed limit (any less, and the cops would have figured I was up to no good), I gripped the wheel hard and rehearsed my lines.

Name?

John Bishop.

Occupation?

Pastor.

Business in Mexico?

Starting a church, then heading up to another church in Chula Vista.

I hit some light traffic. Sitting there, running through the lines one more time, it struck me that none of my answers were lies. Not *really*. John Bishop was (and still is) my real name. I actually was a minister. And I was going to get back to Chula Vista . . . eventually.

That third answer, though. That one was a real doozy.

In a sense, I *had* been on a religious mission. Almost every day in Mexico, I'd talked to someone from the cartel about God. They'd come to me in my small rented apartment and sit at my kitchen table, asking for guidance. They'd confess that they'd been unfaithful to their wives or that they'd strayed from what they believed to be the righteous path in life. I always tried to give them good advice and to instruct them in the ways of Jesus.

When one of them was gunned down or stabbed in the streets—which happened more often than you'd think—I ran the funerals, saying prayers over their bodies as they were lowered into the ground. When the funerals were over, I would comfort their wives, friends, and children.

But that wasn't why the cartel kept me around, and I knew it.

To them I wasn't a religious leader. I was just the fat, unassuming gringo who, as often as they wanted me to, was willing to climb into a busted-up, drug-filled Volkswagen Passat, drive it over the border into California, and sit at a diner for about four hours while some cartel guys drove the car away, unloaded it, and brought it back. Then, at some point down the line, I would collect about $50,000 for my troubles.

Which, you have to admit, wasn't a bad rate for a few hours of driving.

Of course, "willing" isn't exactly the right word. More than once over the past few months, my superiors had made it clear that I didn't really have a choice in the matter. They'd come in, place a loaded gun on the table—the same table we'd sit at while discussing matters of religion and spirituality—and remind me of the "significant debts" that I owed the organization. They'd remind me that I had been enjoying their protection from rival gangs and that a whole lot of bad things could happen to me if I ever stopped cooperating. They'd remind me that my work for the cartel allowed those bad things to be forgotten.

They'd reminded me, in short, that I had no friends, no family, and no place else to go.

Trust me, I always wanted to tell them. *No one knows that better than I do.*

Five years earlier my life had been pretty good. I was preaching to crowds of thousands every Sunday morning. My church, Living Hope, had gotten so big that we had to rent out an old Kmart in the middle of Vancouver, Washington, to accommodate the flock. I'd ministered to everybody, including misfits and outcasts of all kinds. We were a church for the people who were not into church—a church for the "rest of us." I welcomed anyone who felt they had nowhere else to turn. Reaching people who were not saved, regardless of race, sexual orientation, addiction, marital status, societal status, or socioeconomic status, was our mission. That meant we welcomed drug dealers, ex-felons, and anyone else who felt they didn't fit in another church. On Easter Sunday back in 2007, I had preached a service to fifteen thousand people, many of whom probably wouldn't have set foot in a church otherwise. I was on top of the world.

Then I blew it.

I cheated. I lied. I squandered the faith that thousands of people had placed in me. By that point, even the luxurious trappings of my new life—the big house, the fancy cars, and the second home in Cabo San Lucas, Mexico—weren't enough to soothe me. I was fired from my position as pastor of the church and chose to take refuge in dark places.

As I pulled up to the checkpoint, memories of those places came to my mind in flashes. I saw dark motel rooms. I saw heroin needles lined up on tables. I saw the face of my son as he lay half dead on the couch of some trap house in the middle of a small Mexican village. Dwelling on these images for too long, I knew, would make me go insane.

So I tried to push them down. I figured there'd be plenty of time to think about all these things—and, most importantly, to begin fixing them—once I got myself over the border and parked the car outside the usual meeting place: a Denny's just off the highway, where the security cameras had some serious blind spots. There I'd sit for a few hours at the counter, just like I'd done dozens of times before. I'd sip coffee and try to figure out the best way to tell the cartel that the ride I just did was my last one. At this point I didn't care what kind of threats they made. I didn't care what they had on me.

I needed to be done.

But first I needed to have one more quick conversation with the thin, tired-looking border patrol agent up ahead.

Heart pounding, I pulled up slowly and rolled down my window, like always. I flashed a smile and tried to ignore the sweat running down my back.

The agent flashed me a weak smile, then asked for my name.

"John Bishop," I said.

So far, so good.

He asked what I was doing in Mexico, and I spit out my line, making sure to pause in all the right places so it didn't seem too rehearsed.

He looked satisfied.

Then, just as I was about to hit the gas and make my way toward Denny's—and freedom—he held up a hand and told me to stop.

Something near the bottom of the car had caught his eye.

My heart jumped into my throat. My hands shook.

I'd heard this story a million times before: The criminal who says he's about to go straight finally gets caught on his last big job. I just didn't think it would ever happen to me.

Then again, no one ever does.

The next few seconds were a blur. The agent stopped traffic in both directions, then waved over a few more guys from the guard station. They ran straight at me in a ragged line, holding their rifles at the ready.

The agent bent down to inspect the car, disappearing from view for a moment. When he came back up, he was holding a greasy brick of weed covered in frayed duct tape.

"Alright," he said. "We got something here. Hands off the wheel, sir. Get out of the car now. Get on your knees."

The agents approached, pointing their rifles straight at my head.

Before I could even try to explain, I was being dragged out of the car by a man with all the finesse of a trash compactor. As he threw me down to the pavement, I could see deep lines of traffic stretching outward in both directions. Drivers leaned their heads out their windows to get a better look at me.

Horns blared. People screamed. All the noise made it hard to hear the orders the agent was shouting at me.

But I'd seen enough action movies to know the gist.

Hands where we can see them. Don't move.

You have the right to remain silent. Anything you say can and will . . .

Sitting there with my knees pressed to the warm asphalt, I tried to calculate exactly how long I was going away for. The sentence, I knew, depended on how much weed was in the car.

Then, for the first time, it hit me. I had no idea how much marijuana was in the car. I didn't even know the sentencing guidelines for people who got caught doing what I did. When I first started trafficking marijuana, someone from the cartel had told me I wouldn't serve more than a single month for each pound of product I was trying to bring across the border. I figured that didn't sound too bad.

But it was a lie.

Just like everything else they told me.

In the moments before the agents violently scooped me up and slapped the cold handcuffs on my wrists, I found myself praying to God.

I needed help to survive what was coming.

Part 1

THE ACCIDENTAL PASTOR

Chapter 1

I have one picture of my father.

It's black and white. In it, my dad, David Bishop, sits awkwardly in a suit. His hands are crossed over one leg, and he's looking at something just out of frame.

I never got to ask him what it was.

On a winter morning in 1967, two days after my fourth birthday, he came by the house to pick me up. My mother and I were living in a small split-level house in Vancouver, Washington, the town that would be my home for the rest of my life. But even before my parents' divorce, my dad had never spent much time there. He was a long-haul truck driver. He spent his days out driving product across state lines and his nights raising hell at local bars. As a young man, he had served in the army.

My memories of him are all quick flashes. I doubt they're even true memories. I see my dad climbing out of his truck in dirty work clothes, carrying a beer and joking around with his friends. I see him with scars on his knuckles and an angry, faraway look on his face. Most of what I've heard about him comes from my family and some guys he used to drink with here in Vancouver.

Almost none of it is good.

Even the good stuff—"He sure could take a punch, though," or "David could drink more than anyone you've ever seen"—isn't all that good.

I don't know what made my mother tell him that he couldn't drive away with me on that day. Maybe she could tell from his breath that he'd been drinking. Maybe she didn't like the fact that his friend, a guy she'd never liked, was sitting shotgun in the car.

Whatever the reason, my normally meek and unassertive mother stood up to her ex-husband, and he peeled away from the scene in his 1962 Chevy Corvair. I didn't see him go. I didn't even learn that he'd come by until late that night, when police came to the house and let my mother know that they'd found his car crunched up against a tree just off a main road called St. John's Road. Both passengers, they said, had died on impact, and the car was totaled. The cops had also found twenty-five empty beer cans on the floor of the car.

I don't remember hearing the news. I don't remember crying. What I do remember is hearing someone—maybe a police officer, maybe my mother—saying that number.

Twenty-five.

Even to a four-year-old, that seemed like too much for two guys to drink by themselves. It was my first indication that Bishop men have trouble "hitting the brakes," as the cops who found my father might have put it.

When we drink, we drink a lot. When we get in fights, we go until the other guy is on the ground. When we build churches, we build them up until the only buildings that can hold our congregations are decommissioned Kmarts. We spontaneously baptize hundreds of people at once during rock 'n' roll–heavy services. We try to give the *most* glory to God that's ever been given by human beings, to lead the *most* people to Jesus that have ever been led to Him at one time, to do the *most* we can do at all times and in all places. We struggle with addictions, both good and bad, because we don't know how to stop.

And then when we go bad, we go all the way bad.

To the barrios and half-deserted streets of Tijuana. To cartel hideouts and run-down motels and stretches of the Mexican desert where hundreds of bullet-riddled bodies sit just beneath our feet.

To hell on earth.

I'm not sure what would have happened to my father if he'd lived beyond the age of twenty-five. Maybe he'd have cleaned up his act, found God, and founded a church, though I doubt it. I suppose it's possible that he would have disappeared on me anyway or that his demons would have led him astray just like mine did with me. I'll never know. David Bishop didn't live long enough to experience the full ride that comes with having the Bishop blood—all the highs and lows, the long arc of ruin and redemption and everything in between.

I did.

And so did my son, born decades after my dad wrapped his car around that tree, named David after the man neither of us ever really knew.

But I'm getting ahead of myself.

If David Bishop had a funeral, I don't remember it.

My dad didn't belong to a church, and neither did my mother. I assume my family found a local pastor to say a few words over my dad's body, inserting his name into the traditional funeral prayer, rushing through the whole affair so he could get out of the room with all those drunks and seedy-looking dealers.

Today we lay to rest David Bishop, who. . . . May God bless . . . Amen.

In my youth, Vancouver wasn't a churchgoing kind of town. More than anything, it was a bedroom community to Portland, Oregon, which sat a few miles away. Small houses were built in neat rows along wide, quiet streets. Strawberry fields dotted the landscape. I'm not sure I ever set foot inside a church—not on purpose, at least. Sometimes, walking with my mother or my grandparents, I'd pass a church on the road and take a quick look.

Watching the people filing out—the men in pressed khakis and button-downs, the women in dresses—I couldn't help noticing that none of them looked happy. They seemed bored. Sleepy. Like they were relieved for the service to be over and done with. I was happy that my mother allowed me and my younger brother, Ron, to spend Sunday mornings running around the house with our action figures instead of squirming around on hard wooden pews in itchy church pants.

To me, God was an old man with a beard who made the world, just like Santa Claus was an old man with a beard who brought you presents on Christmas if you were good. Heaven was a place in the clouds where my dad went when he died. Beyond that, I didn't think much about faith. I didn't know there was a God I could pray to for relief.

My dad was laid to rest in a cemetery on the far side of town. I never visited his grave. When my friends at school asked about my dad, I'd tell them he drove his car into a tree and died. They'd look at me like I'd just told them he flew to Jupiter on a flying hot dog. I don't blame them. Most kids, if they're lucky, don't have to learn about death until they've had almost a decade of life on earth—and even then it's because of an elderly grandparent who passes away peacefully, not changing their lives much in the process. They don't grow up with a hole in the middle of their lives the way my brother and I did.

We didn't think much about it at the time. I would see kids leaving for camping trips with their dads or standing out in their driveways fixing cars with their dads, and I'd think about my own dad—picturing him with a straight face and a suit on, looking out at something the way he was doing in that single photograph I had of him.

But the feeling that came over me when I thought of my father wasn't sadness. It was more like emptiness. At four years old I didn't understand the difference between a dad who leaves on purpose and one who dies in an accident. To me, it felt like my father abandoned me. No amount of kind words from my mother or time spent outside with my friends could make me forget that. I missed my dad, and I didn't understand why he had to die. I had no God to pray to for relief.

This would have been a good time for a positive role model to step into my life and show me a path forward. Maybe a good teacher or a pastor. If I'd met one, I might have avoided a few big mistakes and dealt with the pain of losing my dad early. Things might have turned out differently for me.

But life didn't throw me a positive male role model.

It threw me Dean.

The first time I saw him, he was standing in the front door of my house in a T-shirt and ripped-up jeans. His hair was long and greasy. He drove a beat-up car with a loud engine.

My dad had been dead for two years. I was six years old, running around the house like a crazy person, hopped up on sugar. Dean seemed to think I was funny. I remember that he made my mama happy, at least in the beginning. She had a great smile, and we hadn't seen it for a few years, what with the divorce and my dad's death and the stress of raising two kids on her own. I was happy to see her enjoying herself with Dean.

In the beginning they'd go out at night and come back late. Then Dean started coming over to the house more and more, leaving his clothes and his belongings around the living room. It wasn't long before I started seeing him at the table every morning, where he'd sit eating cereal, mostly ignoring me. I used to tell stories and jokes to impress him. I'd ask him to take me places, and he'd say,

"Maybe later," or sometimes no. Ron, who was still a toddler at the time, annoyed Dean with his crying. But he didn't lose his temper, at least not in the beginning.

Dean and my mama were married in a small ceremony a few years after they met. I stood up at the altar with them and smiled, just like I was supposed to.

We moved into a house he owned a few miles from our old one. In the backyard Dean grew marijuana plants, harvesting his crop every few days and selling the product in bulk around town. He kept shotguns in almost every corner of the house, knowing that the plants out back—and more importantly, the cash they brought in—made him a prime target for robberies. My mother still seemed happy for a while, at least in front of me and my brother. All her life, she tried her best to hide her troubles from us.

But soon those troubles came out into the open. Dean and my mama started getting in knock-down, drag-out fights. She'd scream at him, and he'd smack her in the face. Once, he walked in on my mother giving me a bath. Water terrified me as a kid, so she'd fill a small cup with water and wash my hair like I was a newborn baby. Something about the sight of it set Dean off.

"What the fuck is this?" he asked, stepping into the bathroom.

"He's scared of drowning," my mom said. "I wash him like this because—"

Dean had me by the neck before she could finish the sentence. I was naked and wet, screaming for help. My mom tried to get me back as he lifted me out of the water, but he could keep her down with ease. When she struggled enough to annoy him, he threw her out of the room and into the wall. She hit it hard enough to leave a large dent in the sheetrock. I heard pictures falling off the walls and glass shattering as Dean walked me over to the toilet and opened the lid. He said he was going to teach me a lesson about being tough.

Then he shoved my face in the bowl.

I smelled rot and urine as the coppery water entered my mouth. I screamed, and the screams echoed back into my ears at twice the volume. Dean asked if I'd had enough. My teeth clanked against the porcelain as I struggled under his catcher's-mitt palm, a feeling of helplessness spreading through my body along with the sharp waves of physical pain.

When I came up for air, I felt sick. My eyes were closed. I braced for another dip in the toilet, expecting Dean to grab me by the neck again. But he was already out in the hallway, beating on my mother for making a hole in his wall, telling her to clean up all the glass from the pictures she'd caused to fall down when she hit the ground.

There were other lessons. I vividly remember sitting in the living room one night, watching my mama attend to Ron, who'd had an accident in his pants. She removed his pants and rolled them up, then left the room for a second to get something else for him to wear. While she was gone, Ron let a little more pee slip out, and it pooled in the corner of the coffee table. Dean, who'd been watching the whole scene from the couch, screamed and grabbed my three-year-old brother by his neck, just like he'd done with me in the tub.

He rubbed Ron's face in the pee like a dog, believing that it would teach him never to do it again. I screamed, and my mom tried to step in when she got back in the room. But she'd learned from the bathroom incident. Rather than jumping on Dean's back and trying to make him stop, she hung back and waited for it to be over, probably feeling the same shame and panic that I did.

That night, I made plans to kill Dean. I thought about what my dad would do to this drug-dealing scumbag if he hadn't died. Although I didn't know much about David Bishop, I knew he was a fighter who didn't take any shit from anyone. I imagined him driving his fists into Dean's face over and over again, tossing him into walls just like he'd done to my mother and making him cry the way he'd made her cry.

Night after night, I dreamed about revenge.

But then I'd wake up, and Dean would still be there. He'd watch me and my brother like a hawk, waiting for us to slip up so he could beat on us again. I wanted to get tall and strong enough to hit him back or at least to resist him. When I was around ten, I started doing push-ups and jumping jacks in my bedroom, trying to build my muscles. I had an older friend who knew how to lift weights, and he started teaching me at the weight room at school.

It was no use. Every time I said a word he didn't like, Dean would whack me again. After a few years of living in his house, my mother walked around like a ghost. She was terrified of making him angry. I don't think I'd ever seen a person so unhappy.

In the end, it wasn't a big, tough guy who rescued my brother and me from that abusive household.

It was a feisty old woman with a booming voice and short gray hair.

My grandmother.

One day, a few hours after one of the worst fights I'd ever seen Dean and my mother have, she showed up at the front door of the house with a shotgun in her hand, cocked and ready to fire. She screamed at Dean, who may or may not have been home, and told us to pack our things and get in the car.

I looked around and realized that my mother had already loaded up most of our stuff. My toys and clothes were in bags. I helped my mom carry what I could out to the car, and we sped off. From the back seat, I heard my mother breathe a sigh of relief.

We were safe.

Dean disappeared.

But not for long.

A few months later he was back in the kitchen of my grandparents' house, eating dinner with us and trying to act like everything was normal. By this point I had begun calling my grandmother Mom and my mother Mama. Sitting at the table, Dean seemed more like his old self—like the guy who'd first come to pick my mother up at our old house rather than the monster who took over once we moved in with him. It was all a lie, of course, but as a kid without a father, I was all too happy to buy into the lie.

Over the next few years, Dean played the role of father figure to me, albeit with a little reluctance. He'd play catch with me in the yard of my grandparents' house and talk to me about my favorite sports teams. At school I started referring to him as my dad—not my stepdad or my mom's husband, just *Dad*.

He wasn't around much. Given all the abuse he'd heaped on my mother, my grandmother kept Dean on a tight leash. He'd come over only when invited, and he'd always be on his best behavior when he did.

When he wasn't around, the house was almost normal. My mother spent most of her time keeping busy, so my grandmother was the one who cared for Ron and me. Her husband, my grandfather, was a quiet, soft-spoken man who worked as a land purchaser for the state of Washington. My brother and I called him Pop. Although my grandmother was the primary disciplinarian (my brother and I never forgot the way she handled that shotgun when she picked us up from Dean's house), Pop provided a calm, steady presence in the household.

Most days I'd wake up in my bedroom at the back of the house and attach myself to him like a barnacle. I'd help him fix cars and mow the lawn and make small repairs around the house. To this day I can see him driving me around in his old car, pointing out all the land in Vancouver that he'd acquired for the state of Washington. Before I was even old enough to wander around on my own, I knew the layout of the town like the back of my hand. I knew the seedy parts and the rich parts, the best places to get pizza and the streets you should avoid walking on at night.

One afternoon Dean called at the last minute to cancel plans with my mother. He was supposed to come over for dinner, but he got tied up "at the office" (whatever that means for a drug dealer). My mother was annoyed by it, but I was inconsolable. No matter how many times I'd watched him beat on my mother, I still thought of Dean as my father. I craved his approval, and every time he failed to show up for dinner, it felt like he was passing a verdict on *me*. Telling me I wasn't worth having as a son. Telling me I wasn't smart enough or interesting enough or tough enough to spend time around. Every time, it felt like a punch to the stomach.

To console me, Pop would drive me around town. Once as we rolled slowly up St. John's Road, I looked out the back window and saw the tree my father had crashed into when I was four. My grandfather was telling me about the housing developments he'd helped build—how hard the deal had been to get done, what the state of Washington's plans for the area were. But all I could focus on were my father's faded black tire tracks, still visible after all these years. I followed them with my eyes from the road to the tree, imagining what it must have been like for my dad to look up, his vision faded from a dozen beers, and see that tree hurtling toward him.

I imagined him squeezing the wheel, swerving at the last moment. His buddy screaming.

Did he know it was the end?

Did it hurt?

Was he thinking about me or my mom?

A few weeks later I rode my bike down to the spot and hopped off. Walking up to the tree, I saw car parts and broken bits of glass that the cops had failed to clean up. I stood there for a while, and I thought about life. My father had spent twenty-five years on earth, and I could count the signs that he'd been here on one hand. There was me, for one thing, and my brother. There was a single photograph and a few sheets of paper from his time in the military.

And there was the ugly, twisted scar on this giant oak tree.

Over the next few years, I'd visit this spot often, always alone. I'd stand there for long stretches of time as the cars passed on St. John's Road, running my hand over the scarred wood, always able to feel the place where my father had collided with it. No matter how much time passed, the bark never fully grew back.

The wound was always open.

Dean's last dinner at my grandmother's house began quietly, as usual.

He stormed in and sat down at the table, waiting to be served. He and my grandmother glared at one another across the table while my mother tried to make everyone get along. She asked Dean how work was going, hoping he'd act like a decent human being and respond with a full sentence.

He usually didn't.

He'd grunt and eat, then complain about someone around town he was having a problem with. I'd try to show him pictures I'd drawn or stage a wrestling match for him with my action figures, and he'd ignore me. When I persisted, he'd listen to me like he was listening to hold music on the phone. But I was determined to get his attention. I wouldn't stop asking him questions, showing him things, telling him about what had happened to me in the weeks—sometimes the months—since he'd last come around my grandparents' house.

I don't know what was said to set him off. Maybe my grandmother made one too many snide remarks in his direction. Maybe my mother told a story that bored him. I suppose it's equally likely that it was me.

All I know is that at some point between dinner and dessert, Dean started screaming. The sound of it brought me right back to the bathroom, where he'd held my head in the toilet while screaming at my mother to stay out. I froze. So did my grandparents. One by one, Dean pointed his finger around the room, delivering his final, expletive-laden verdicts about all of us. I can't print most of them here, especially the ones about my grandmother and my mother.

I braced, waiting for my turn to feel Dean's wrath. But he skipped me and my brother. To him, we weren't even worth screaming at. He put his hands under the heavy wooden table and lifted it, sending all the plates, drinks, silverware, and food crashing to the ground. I got bits of mashed potato all over my shirt.

At the sound of the front door slamming, I managed to unfreeze for long enough to follow Dean out to the yard.

I wanted him to say *something* to me, even if it was goodbye.

Sprinting, I called his name. He didn't turn around. When he finally realized I wasn't going to go away, he turned around and walked toward me, then whacked me in the center of my chest with his palm. I felt the wind come out of me as I hit the ground.

"Dad," I said, using the name I'd been using for him with my friends for so many years now. "Please don't leave me."

Dean leaned down and shook his finger in my face.

"You are not my kid, and you never were," he said. "I am not your dad. Get over it."

I cried.

Dean got in the car and drove away.

I never saw him again.

Chapter 2

"Get him, Johnny!"

"Hands up!"

"Kill him!"

A few years later I stood in a backyard, wobbling after my fifth hard punch to the head that night. My shirt was off. My hands were swollen and scraped at the knuckles. I looked around, trying to see who was cheering for me. But I couldn't see anything.

I could barely tell where I was anymore.

I charged forward, hands over my face, and ducked another punch. The kid in front of me was breathing heavily, wobbling almost as badly as I was. He dropped his hands long enough for me to get a clean shot at his jaw.

I took it.

He stumbled backward, and I charged at him, fists flying at his bare midsection. If we were in a boxing ring, he'd have been on the ropes. But out here in my uncle's yard, there was nothing to hit but a crowd of other shirtless, testosterone-filled teenage boys, all waiting for their turn to step into the ring and beat on each other. He fell back on them, and they pushed him back into the ring.

Into *me*.

I pummeled him with both hands again.

My Uncle Jim, sitting nearby on a lawn chair with a can of beer in his hand, cheered me on.

"There you go, Johnny."

"Harder!"

"You got him! Keep it up!"

The kid—whose face now runs together with the faces of all the other kids I beat on between the ages of about ten and thirteen—went down. I heard his body hit the mud with a squishing noise. The breath left his body just like mine had when Dean knocked me to the ground outside my grandmother's house and left me for the last time. He might have cried. I don't remember. All I remember is the sound of all those people yelling at me at once, telling me how to hit, cheering me on as I beat on kids from all over Portland, Oregon. It was a small crowd, but still a crowd. I loved it.

And in true Bishop fashion, one fight was never enough.

Neither was a dozen fights.

No matter how many guys I knocked out, I wanted more.

For as long as I've been talking, I've been fighting.

I remember punching someone for the first time when I was about four years old. Some other kid and I had gotten in an argument about a toy we both wanted, and we solved it with our fists. The adults didn't stop us.

When they had problems, they tended to solve things the same way.

In Vancouver, and sometimes in nearby Portland, fistfights were almost as common as conversations. At least they were in my part of the neighborhood. When one of my uncles took the last beer from the cooler and another one got upset about it, they'd usually roll around on the ground for a while, and then one of them would go out to buy more beer. They weren't surprised when the kids around them began acting the same way.

I don't know which one first had the idea of starting up a

bare-knuckle boxing circuit in the backyard. All I know is that one day, I heard I was going to fight a kid from around the corner who was about two heads taller than me with a chest the size of a Maytag refrigerator. I wasn't scared. After so many years of getting beaten on by a full-sized adult, a kid my age couldn't scare me. It didn't matter how tough-looking and muscular he was. I walked out to the yard and traded punches with the kid, surprised at how easy it was for me to put him down.

I've heard there are musicians in the world who can play symphonies before they've had a single piano lesson, and painters who can nail a landscape the first time they sit down at the canvas. That's how it was with me and fighting. I wasn't some great technician like Muhammad Ali or Floyd Mayweather, and I didn't necessarily have Mike Tyson–like power either. But I could step up to anyone—even guys two times my size—and never feel an ounce of fear. And like so much else in life, fighting is about confidence.

By the time I was about twelve years old, I'd won the backyard bare-knuckle boxing championship so many times that I could have become a millionaire from the prize money. But there was no prize money. There was only the satisfaction of knowing that I was the toughest kid on the block, and the acceptance of my uncles, who seemed to like the idea that their nephew was becoming a little ass-kicker just like them.

Every time I stepped into the ring—or, more accurately, the circle of shirtless kids in the dirt—I'd listen for the voice of my Uncle Jim, telling me to hit harder and duck punches. I'd get high on the thought that people were cheering for me, watching me, getting a little relief from the problems of their own lives for a few minutes by kicking back with a beer and watching me fight. It was probably during one of these fights when I first realized that I had a knack for entertaining people. I grew to love the sound of applause that came whenever I landed a good hit. I craved approval from the bigger kids, and I earned it by never walking away from a fight. Soon I had friends all over Portland who'd heard tales of my prowess in the ring.

Over time I developed a set of rules about fighting that I would keep for decades. Although I never wrote them down, they were always in my head.

First, I never beat on anyone smaller than me.

Second, I never walked away from a fight; it didn't matter if the guy was twice my size and three times my weight, which was the case with a lot of the guys I stepped in the ring with. I would always approach him with my fists up, my chin tucked, and my feet planted firmly on the ground, ready for action.

Third, and most importantly, I beat on every bully I could get my hands on. When I saw a big guy picking on a smaller guy—even if I didn't know either one of them, even if I had somewhere else to be—I'd put my nose right in the big guy's face and ask why he didn't pick on someone his own size. And I'd whale on him until he was bloody and crying. I know now that Dean reminded me of bullies, and bullies reminded me of Dean.

To this day, there's something about a bully that sets my teeth on edge.

At school I was a menace.

I'd cut class and mouth off to teachers. My report cards, some of which I still have, contain mostly A's and B's, but they also contain comments about how I could not, for the life of me, sit still or shut up. If something wasn't nailed down, I'd steal it. There were teachers who tried to intervene, but I didn't want to listen to them. My friends and I spent most of our time in the weight room, trying to figure out how to grow our muscles so we could fight better.

Which we did. A lot.

I don't think I can count the times I was dragged through

the hallway by my ear after getting in a scrape with a classmate. Every time, the principal would call my poor grandparents, who'd taken me on as a kind of surrogate son. So it was usually my grandmother—Mom to me—who'd have to come down to school and deal with whatever mess I'd made. That usually meant a lot of screaming and cursing on the way home, followed by some kind of punishment.

Sometimes, the job of picking me up fell to Pop, who'd pull up in his car, collect me, and do very little other than shake his head and sigh.

"John Boy," he'd say, "what the hell are you getting up to now?"

And that'd be it.

On some level I understood just how much of an inconvenience I was to my grandparents. They'd raised their only daughter, gotten her out of the house, and prepared for a life of solitude, only to have my mother and her two kids storm in and throw everything out of whack again. Suddenly they were looking after a little hell-raiser, only now they had a fraction of the stamina they'd had the first time around. My grandmother dealt with this by losing her patience a lot, snapping at me every time I put a toe out of line. Pop tended to stay quiet, hoping things would work out in the end.

As I got older, I spent less time in the house and more out on the streets.

There I found even more trouble.

"Whose blood is that?"

Uncle Jim stood in the hallway of his house, staring at me. It was a weekday afternoon in 1975. I'd just walked in wearing a brand-new purple shirt. It was shiny and soft, with wide lapels and big buttons, like something John Travolta had worn in *Saturday Night Fever*.

And it was covered in blood.

Uncle Jim asked again. "Whose is it, Johnny?"

"Mine," I said.

Which, in his household, where I stayed most weekdays when my grandparents got tired of me, was a bad answer.

He asked what had happened, and I filled him in as best I could. I told him I'd been walking down the street in my new shirt—a gift from my mother—thinking I was the coolest kid on the block. Hell, I might have been *dancing*, for how woman's-man-no-time-to-talk awesome I thought I looked. Then I ran into a kid named Robert from around the corner, whose parents were recent immigrants from Mexico. He told me I was wearing a girl's shirt and squared up to me. So I gave him a couple punches to the head, and he gave me a couple right back.

"We went at it for a while," I explained to Uncle Jim, "and I landed a couple good hits. We went to the ground and wrestled a little. He hit me here, and I guess it bled pretty good."

I pointed to my nose and recapped some other injuries, just like I might have done after one of my sanctioned backyard brawls.

Uncle Jim nodded.

"What then?" he asked.

I must have looked confused, because he asked again.

"What happened then, Johnny?"

"I, uh, walked away," I said. "And now I'm here."

"Covered in your own blood," he said.

I looked down and shrugged.

"Well . . . yeah. I guess."

Uncle Jim walked toward me slowly, raising his finger so it was level with my face. I could smell beer and cigarettes on his breath.

"You march your ass right down there, Johnny," he said, enunciating every word, "and you kick the living shit out of this kid. You do it so he can't get up. And you make sure you do it right out in his front yard, so everyone in this whole fucking neighborhood can see, so that no one ever messes with you, or any other member of my family, again."

He shoved me out the door, and I was walking back toward Robert's house before I could even begin to process the conversation. As my feet moved over the asphalt, I thought of all the stories I'd heard about my dad.

"He was small," someone had told me, "but holy shit, he and your Uncle Jim would fight anyone, anytime. It didn't matter *how* big they were. Especially if someone trashed their family. You did not want to mess with your dad."

Before I knew it, I was knocking on Robert's door, seeing his mother's scared face as she peeked out to see who it was.

She called behind her for Robert, and he appeared. He was a little taller than me, a little darker. He was still covered in spots of blood from our tussle earlier. He looked tired. Worn out. For a moment, there was a sorrowful look in his eye, as if he wanted to apologize and put the whole thing behind him.

I heard Uncle Jim's voice in my head. *Do it out in his front yard, where everyone . . .*

I shoved Robert and backed up. He followed me out into the yard, shoving me and throwing punches. We backed up, shifting on our feet like boxers. Suddenly he was climbing the black wrought iron lamppost in the corner of the yard by the street, scaling it like a Mexican Spider-Man as he prepared to kick me in the face.

Which he did.

I stumbled, pouring more blood onto my purple shirt. Robert jumped off the pole and came at me, but I got in a good hit to the stomach, and he went down hard. My vision went blurry as I climbed on top of him and threw punches like my life depended on it. Sitting on his chest, I regained my composure, even as I was running out of breath from swinging my arms into Robert's face.

I whacked him on the chin, and something snapped.

I whacked him in the eye, and blood came out from under the lid.

I punched, and punched, and punched some more.

Thinking about what Uncle Jim would do. What my dad would do.

When I stopped, it wasn't because I thought Robert had had enough. It wasn't because he was crying or spitting out blood, though he was. It was because I was tired. (One thing no one tells you about fighting is that it's a pretty cardio-intensive activity; most guys have only about twenty or thirty seconds in them.)

I left Robert lying on his lawn and walked home.

I thought I heard his mother scream as she came out of the house to care for him.

When I walked back into my uncle's house, Uncle Jim was sitting in a chair in the living room, watching television. He glanced back at me, his eyes going wide as he noticed the pools of blood on my shirt, the splatters on my face.

"Whose blood is that?" he said.

I looked at myself in the hallway mirror, proud of what I saw. My hands felt like I'd just dropped cinderblocks on them. My chin ached where Robert had punched me.

I turned back to Uncle Jim.

"His."

He got up, patted me on the shoulder, and opened the fridge for another beer.

"Good boy," he said. "Now let's watch a movie."

Chapter 3

About a year later, after a few hundred more fights and almost as many near suspensions from school, I met the person who'd change my life forever.

It was a summer afternoon in 1979. I was standing in the middle of the tiny music room at Hudson Bay High School, singing "Time in a Bottle" by Jim Croce. Beside me a girl named Kelly accompanied me on the piano, hitting all the minor chords in all the right places, helping me out with the melody by picking it out with her left hand. Even the chorus, which got a little high for my range, wasn't much trouble.

"But there never seems to be enough time, to do the things you want to do, once you find them . . ."

I'd been in jazz choir for about three years. Other than brawling and lifting weights, singing was my favorite thing in the world to do. This was especially true on days when there was a small crowd of kids in the choir room, all hanging out and listening to one another practice their solos while Kelly accompanied us on the piano.

That day there was a new face in the room: a bright, shining one framed by blond hair.

I climbed down off the cheap metal risers and walked straight toward her, needing to know her name. It felt like we were the only two people in the tiny music room. I learned she was Kelly's sister, who'd skipped school for the afternoon to listen to her play piano.

Michelle.

We talked for a while as the other kids sang their solos, mostly '70s folk and soft rock—James Taylor, Gordon Lightfoot, Fleetwood Mac. Right away I was struck by Michelle's beauty and the way she smiled when telling a story.

I wanted to talk to her for hours. To be alone with her.

To marry her.

The bell rang. I asked when I could see her again. She said she was turning sixteen on the first day of July and told me there'd be a birthday party in downtown Vancouver, at the community center.

"You should come," she said.

I told her I'd be there.

I was riding high. I think I managed to get through the rest of the afternoon without punching anyone or stealing anything, which was big for me. In the weeks that remained in the school year, I hounded Kelly for information about Michelle. She didn't give me much, so I asked around.

"Her stepdad is friends with the mayor," someone told me. "He runs the parks and rec department. She's *very* religious."

I didn't think much about that last part. I barely knew what it meant. All I knew was that I liked this girl, and I was going to her birthday party. I just needed to make it out of tenth grade—which I did, by the skin of my teeth—and survive the early summer in my neighborhood.

By this point I was lifting weights every day. There was a gym in town where my friends and I spent almost all our free time. Every morning in the summer we'd head over and throw weights around until we literally couldn't walk anymore. One of my buddies had a book by Arnold Schwarzenegger called *Pumping Iron*, a collection of everything the Big Man had learned about bodybuilding.

We treated every line in that book—and everything Arnold said—as gospel. It was the closest thing any of us had to a Bible. Arnold wrote that you needed to eat more protein than anything else, and to eat so much that you ended up in a caloric surplus after training. And so we hoovered all the steak, eggs, and grilled chicken we could get our hands on. Arnold said you had to train every muscle to failure on every set, moving past the point where you were shaking and howling in pain. So we did that too. Every day, I'd leave the gym wobbling from all the squats I'd done, happy I was getting bigger and stronger with each rep.

We also went off-book. At some point that summer, a buddy of mine walked into the gym with a plastic baggie. He opened it, revealing syringes and small bottles of clear liquid. "This," he told me, "will take you to the next level, Johnny."

Steroids.

Strange as it might sound, shooting myself full of this stuff never felt like doing drugs. It felt the same as eating all that protein and drinking all that water: just helping my torn-up muscles repair themselves and grow back stronger. Maybe that's because the side effects—mostly aggression and foggy-headedness—came on slowly, over a period of weeks rather than minutes and hours.

That summer my friends and I partied more than ever. We'd go through cases of beer in a matter of hours. My memories of that time involve mostly chains and weights, meat and raw eggs, empty parking lots and dingy basements. The night before Michelle's birthday party, when I was getting a little nervous about seeing her again, I went out drinking with the guys, and we decided it'd be a good idea to shave our heads.

Naturally, I went first. My friend got behind me with an electric razor and lopped my shoulder-length blond hair right off. By the time the cold metal touched my head for the fourth or fifth time, I started to think head-shaving was a bad idea. But it was too late. Once the first big strip comes off, you're all the way in.

I caught my reflection in a window and felt a flutter of fear. I looked like Mr. Clean. But my friends all shaved their heads in solidarity, and we did a bunch of push-ups to celebrate.

The next morning we worked out hard. I did sets of heavy squats with chains on the bar, then leg extensions and leg presses. My thighs felt like they were on fire. I spotted all five of my friends as they worked through the same circuit, yelling words of encouragement and playing hard rock songs through the gym speakers. We drank water and raw eggs. We shot up steroids.

Then it was party time.

The thought that bringing a group of friends to a nice girl's birthday party—one to which I had clearly been invited out of pity and awkwardness in the first place—was impolite did not occur to me. Neither did the fact that with our shaved heads and sleeveless bodybuilding T-shirts, we looked like a gang of jacked-up white supremacists who'd just busted out of prison. Together we headed down to the Marshall Center, a collection of sports courts and event spaces right in the center of Vancouver, and poked around until we found the party.

As soon as I stepped up to the front door, I could tell something was off. Everywhere I looked, there was a pair of wide, concerned eyes staring back at me. Women clutched their purses. Men looked around, wondering if everyone else was seeing what they were seeing.

Inside the room, standing in a dress by a table filled with paper plates and presents, was Michelle.

I wanted to talk to her. And I wanted everyone else in the room to disappear and leave us alone.

I stood for a moment in the doorway with my friends and watched a guy come up to Michelle. He pointed in my direction and asked her something. She squinted and shook her head.

"No," I thought I heard her say. "Don't know them."

And why would she?

Standing there on that summer afternoon, I looked absolutely nothing like that calm, blond-haired kid she'd seen singing "Time in a Bottle" all those weeks ago.

The guy (her brother Mike, it turned out) approached and asked me to leave and to take my friends with me. My first instinct—the one that comes before thought, which usually drove my every action—told me to shove him and start a fight. But something, I don't know what, took over, and I nodded.

I might have even *apologized*, which was a first.

My friends and I left the party. I didn't even look back.

That summer Uncle Jim worked long days at Burlington Northern Railroad. I was spending more and more time at his house by this point, mostly because my grandparents couldn't quite keep up with me. When he was home, he kept a close eye on me. While he was at work, though, I was free to roam the streets at will. It felt good not to have a guy looking over my shoulder, imposing his hyper-masculine code of honor on me. One day, while he was working, I went back to Robert's house, shuddering a little at the sight of the lamppost he'd climbed up to try to kick me.

I knocked on the door.

He answered, probably looking around for a crowd. But there was no one else. I apologized for what had transpired between us, not making any excuses. For some reason I felt that apologizing to him was important. I also knew it was important that Uncle Jim never find out that I was doing it.

Robert took it well. At least, as well as you can take an apology from a guy who beat you bloody in front of the whole neighborhood.

We parted as friends, and I learned a lesson about myself—my *true* self. When the crowds weren't there and there was no one pushing me to do something, I had a real heart for people. And it had nothing to do with violence.

Of course, the world is full of crowds. And, as I would soon learn, tuning them out—and being your true self—isn't so easy.

Chapter 4

I find it kind of amazing that I went on to become a full-time criminal. I've always kind of sucked at crime.

Sure, there were a few early thefts that went well. I nabbed packs of gum and some shirts from a local department store. I got pretty good at small-time theft.

But as soon as the stakes got high, I screwed up and got caught. *Every* time. To this day, I remember walking into a shop in downtown Vancouver when I was about twelve and grabbing items off the shelves, thinking the lady shopkeeper couldn't see me. Then, before I could run out of the store with the loot, she was standing in my way—all five foot two, 105 pounds of her—telling me I needed to pay for my items or put them back.

I ran, looking for a back door.

There wasn't one.

"The cops are on their way," she said. "You are *not* leaving."

"Lady! You called the *cops*?"

For the next ten minutes she chased me around the store like a cartoon cat chasing a mouse. I picked up boxes of cereal and threw them in her direction. She called me names so foul that even I had never heard them. I almost got around her once, but she boxed me in like an NBA power forward. To anyone watching from outside, the scene would have looked ridiculous. I was almost the same size as this woman and nearly double her weight. I could have shoplifted *her*, thrown her over my shoulder, and run a mile without breaking a sweat.

But I didn't want to hurt anyone. There was no way I'd shove a woman, even as a crazy kid. So I ran, and ran some more, hoping she'd get tired and give me a way out before the cops came.

The cops showed up, made me put all the stuff back, and put me in the back of their car. Probably wanting to save themselves some paperwork, they drove me right back to my grandparents' house, where Pop was waiting. He talked to them at the front door, promising to keep a better eye on me and punish me accordingly.

"John Boy," he said, shaking his head. "What are you doing out there?"

If the question was supposed to make me feel guilty about my actions, it didn't work. It only made me want to come up with better schemes.

Once, when I was about fourteen, I traveled with the jazz choir to an amphitheater up north. We performed a set of pop songs for a small audience, and it went well. I sang along with the rest of the choir with a big smile on my face.

But the entire time I was onstage, all I could think about was the dressing room in back. We'd traveled up with the band and the orchestra, who'd stashed their instruments in the dressing room after they performed. Each one, I figured, was worth a few hundred bucks. And I knew there was a pawn shop in town that bought and sold musical instruments.

What could go wrong?

I snuck backstage after the concert and grabbed a flute. It was the only instrument I could stuff down my pants before getting back onto the bus. The next day, I walked into the pawn shop and plopped it on the counter, barely noticing the SCHOOL PROPERTY stamp right on the back of the case.

"Where'd you get this?" the guy asked, raising an eyebrow.

"Don't remember."

"You want to sell it?"

"Yep."

"Let me go make a call."

He walked to the back of the store, and I waited at the counter, in my head already spending the cash I was about to get. I figured the flute was good for at least a hundred bucks, which I'd soon turn into protein shakes, baseball cards, or whatever else I was into at the time.

In back, the guy made two phone calls. The first was to Pop—who, it turned out, was an old friend of his—and the second (on Pop's advice) was to the cops. When he came back out, he seemed to want to chat a lot about flutes, music, the weather, my time at school. It never occurred to me that he was stalling.

After a few minutes he sighed and said he couldn't make the deal. I was about to argue when the bell above the door rang and two uniformed officers walked right through it. In my memory they're the same two cops who'd picked me up outside the lady's store, but I'm sure they were different. After a while the faces of the cops all started to blend in my head. That single face was always tired, slightly annoyed, and dispirited. They hated picking me up almost as much as I hated getting picked up.

Looking back, I can see how hopeless it must have seemed to them: another member of the Bishop family falling into addiction and violence, heading straight for prison or death. If nothing else, it was probably exhausting. And boring.

This time, they took me to juvenile detention. Looking around, I saw guys I recognized. Not *exactly* recognized, mind you. Just types of guys I'd grown up around. I got a sense that no matter what I did with my life—no matter how hard I tried to make something of myself—there was a good chance that I'd end up here, in jail, having committed one too many botched robberies or killed the wrong guy accidentally in a fight.

I didn't want it to happen, but something told me it was inevitable.

Pop pulled up a few hours later in his old beat-up Galaxy 500, and I climbed into the passenger seat. He explained that he was the one who'd suggested the pawn shop owner call the cops because he wanted to scare me straight. He told me I needed to stop heading down the road I was on or something bad was going to happen to me.

"I'm worried about you, John Boy," he said, seeming to mean it.

"I know."

We drove off, passing the spot where my father had died, and went home.

During the worst times of my adolescence, I always had the gym. That was where I went to blow off steam, to laugh with my buddies, and to feel like I was making progress at *something* in my life, even if that something was only the size of my pecs, shoulders, and thighs.

By the time I turned seventeen, I was ready for serious competition. All over the Northwest, there were small bodybuilding contests that kids could enter. You'd cut weight, get spray-tanned, and pose in front of a panel of judges. The best physique won. As soon as I found out these contests existed, I became single-minded in my pursuit of a bodybuilding title. By this point I'd seen the film version of *Pumping Iron* dozens of times, and I wanted to win a trophy for being the baddest, strongest man in the room, just like Arnold Schwarzenegger had.

I doubled my protein intake. I started sleeping at the gym. I cycled on and off steroids. By the time my first competition—a relatively small one in town—rolled around, I was a lean 170 pounds of pure muscle. I slept with a garbage bag wrapped around my body so I'd sweat out any excess water weight, and I watched my diet like I'd never watched anything in my life.

The only thing I *didn't* do was cardio. Back then, we were worried that long runs like Sylvester Stallone had done in *Rocky* would eat up precious muscle. So we lifted heavy and short, driving ourselves to the point of failure with all the weight we could handle. I was benching over three hundred pounds and squatting over four hundred with ease. My legs looked like tree trunks. In the days leading up to the contest, I'd stop drinking water altogether, taking only a few sips every day so I wouldn't die. I'd heard this would really make the muscles pop.

It worked. By the morning of the first contest, my skin was tight, and the veins were visible under a thin layer of dried-out skin. I looked like a million bucks. But I felt like hell. Unlike other sports, which require athletes to be in top shape on competition day, bodybuilding demands the opposite. By the time a guy gets onstage, he's been starving himself for at least a few months, and he's probably foregone water for a while too. A stiff wind would blow him right over.

I wobbled a little as I walked into the auditorium where the contest would be held. I was shocked by how many people were crowded into the place. There were cameras, spectators, and a table of judges from big gyms all over the Northwest. Near the stands I saw a girl named Cheryl waving at me. She'd been hanging around my friends and me for a while, hoping to date me. Although I thought she was a nice girl, I didn't feel the same way. She just didn't seem to be my style.

As I approached, I noticed that someone familiar was standing with her.

At first I thought it was my water-starved brain playing tricks on me, throwing up mirages in the gym like it was a desert. But I got closer, still moving unsteadily on my feet, and saw that I wasn't hallucinating at all.

There, dressed in jeans and a white sweater, blond hair falling over her shoulders in waves, was Michelle.

I recognized her right away.

We got to talking, and I heard a voice in the back of my mind: *I'm going to marry this girl.*

I went up onstage that day and posed my butt off, knowing Michelle was watching from the crowd. I don't know if seeing me all jacked up and woozy in a red Speedo was great for her, but it must have been better than seeing the pale skinhead version of me who'd shown up to her sixteenth birthday party.

At the end of the contest I stood on the stage with one eye on Michelle. The announcer called my name, and I went up to give the crowd a wave. There were no trophies or prizes, but the honor was enough. The first thing I did when I got offstage was walk up to Michelle and invite her back to my small apartment in the city, where I'd moved when I turned eighteen.

Much to my surprise, she accepted. She and Cheryl followed me home.

Once we got there, my friends and I began to celebrate my victory. The alcohol began flowing, although Michelle never had a drop of it. But I had enough for both of us, given that the contest was finally over and I could afford to blow off some steam. After a few shots and countless beers, I started thinking it'd be funny to smash something over my head.

I looked around.

The only object I had was a large, old-fashioned A&W Root Beer mug, the kind with the thick glass handle and the small divots up the sides. In my memory it weighs close to twenty pounds, but I'm sure it was more like five. I don't know whether I said anything before I smashed it. All I remember is doing it, getting a laugh, and seeing blood.

Lots of blood, even for me.

But the party didn't stop. I got some more high fives, some more laughs. I got another beer and tried to sop up the flow of blood with a towel from the bathroom. When I looked around for Michelle, she wasn't there. At first I figured, *Whatever. She probably wanted to take a walk because she couldn't handle me and the guys.* I downed my beer and filled up another one. By the time I was halfway through it, Michelle had reappeared in the doorway, only now she was holding a Bible from her car.

It was slightly tattered and faded, as if she'd spent many long hours reading it. I could almost see her fingermarks on the leather. She sat cross-legged on the floor, guys still screaming, music still playing from speakers beside her, and cracked it open. Then she began reading aloud.

Now, considering that I would go on to become a pastor, I would love to say that this was the moment when I allowed the Word of God to enter my heart and change me for the better. I would love to say that I heard a verse that would later become one of my favorites, or that I heard the still small voice of the Lord that very night.

But that's not what happened.

What *did* happen was that we all stared at Michelle for a moment, listening to the unwavering, self-assured tone of voice she used to read the Gospels, and gave each other a look, half *how cute is that* and half *what is wrong with this chick?* I don't remember anything about the specific verses she read or how long she kept reading. I had lost a lot of blood. All I remember is looking at her and feeling a soft, fluttery feeling in my chest, along with a total certainty that I was going to marry her someday.

Later that night, we ended up with Cheryl and one other guy at a Denny's in Vancouver, sitting across a table near the window, eating pancakes and drinking coffee well into the night. Four hours later, while the janitor swept up around us and our waiter stood impatiently against the wall, Michelle and I were still there, talking. I learned about her family and her hobbies. I learned that she'd always had a vague idea that she'd become a pastor's wife someday.

I also learned that Michelle would not, under any circumstances, date me. She didn't want to do that to Cheryl, who she knew liked me. I told her that didn't make sense, because I had never dated Cheryl. But she wouldn't relent. Looking back, I'm sure there was more to it than not wanting to upset a friend. By all objective measures, I was an insane person. No woman in her right mind—especially not one with a family that enjoyed such high standing in the community—would agree to date me right away.

Luckily, my all-in personality didn't only apply to drinking and fighting and building my body.

It also applied to love.

For the next few months, I followed Michelle everywhere, always keeping a respectful distance, always trying to make her laugh. I was obsessed with her, thinking about her all the time. I called Cheryl and begged her to release me from the weird, nonexistent ball-and-chain situation she had me in. At some point I learned that Michelle was working at Kinney Shoes on Grand Boulevard in Vancouver. I would pull up in my car and sit in the parking lot, watching her work—something that seemed sweet at the time but feels a little creepy in hindsight. But I couldn't help it. I was infatuated.

Finally she relented. I think it had something to do with the fact that Cheryl, tired of my phone calls, went to Michelle and said, "Please date him! I can't take this anymore." And from then on, we were almost inseparable. When I was with her, I didn't drink. I didn't fight. I didn't need to do any of the things that I'd been doing to deal with the pain of losing my dad. All I needed to do was talk to her and I'd be happy. Things were changing, and I liked the feeling.

A few weeks after Michelle and I reconnected, I went alone to an outdoor party at a place called Beer Bottle Beach. This was a small stretch of sand on the banks of the Columbia River, a little west of Vancouver. There were kegs of beer, pickup trucks parked in a row, and music blaring from big speakers.

I showed up completely sober, wearing a jacket monogrammed with the logo of our bodybuilding club. Things went well for a while. I had another bodybuilding contest coming up, so I wasn't drinking at all. But I didn't need to. Walking around knowing that Michelle was out in the world waiting for me made me feel more hopped-up than any substance ever had.

Then, out of nowhere, a kid I didn't recognize came up and shoved me. I told him to back off, but he said he'd heard I was tough, and he wanted to see for himself. I looked at my friends, then back at the kid.

Everyone but him seemed to know what was coming.

"You don't want to do this, man," I said. "How about I get you a beer and we settle—"

Before I could finish, his fist was flying at my face.

I ducked it, but barely, and he got in another hit near my ribs. After a few punches back and forth, I got him in a headlock, and my fighter's instincts took over. I pummeled him, just like I'd done to Robert. Just like I'd done to so many other people over the years. He screamed, going limp in my arms, and I let him fall to the floor.

As he gathered himself, my friends clapped me on the back and gave me high fives. They told me that what I'd done was awesome.

Most of the time this kind of affirmation felt good. I didn't usually get pats on the back, so I tended to take them where I could get them. This time, it made me feel completely alone.

I don't remember what made me take a walk alone that night. It might have been something about the way the kid I'd just beaten on had looked as he slunk away from the fight. In any case, I found him leaning against a tree, hugging his own knees with a dazed look on his face. A small stream of blood was running from his eye down his cheek, collecting on his T-shirt. By now the wind coming off the water had picked up; it was probably close to forty degrees. I approached with my hands up and asked how he was doing.

"Fine," he said.

Before I knew it, I was taking off my bodybuilding-club coat and draping it over the kid's shoulders. He winced, backing away slightly. But once he realized this wasn't a trick so I could pummel him some more, he took the coat and thanked me. We stood there for a moment, neither of us speaking. I didn't apologize for what I'd done to him. He didn't apologize for starting the fight.

"Here," I told him. "Take this."

I reached into my pocket and pulled out twenty-eight dollars and some loose change. Everything I had to my name at the time. He took it, and I asked him if there was anything else I could do.

"No," he said. "But thank you."

I stood there alone in my T-shirt, watching him walk up the hill and begin to make his way home on foot. A few minutes later he was gone, and I was thinking about all the high fives I'd gotten for kicking the crap out of him earlier that night. It occurred to me that I had been working my whole life to become the guy no one could beat on—the person everyone was afraid to mess with, who could take down bullies and dispatch troublemakers like Dean, Robert, and the kid I'd just beaten on with ease.

But it didn't feel good.

Handing that kid all the money in my pocket and draping my jacket over his shoulders, though, felt good. And it wasn't because it made me look like a good guy in front of other people. In fact, I don't even think I told anyone I did it when I rejoined the party. It felt good because it was the first sign that there was a good person lurking inside me, albeit one who had to fight with my demons every day to get out.

But as I made my way home that night, my head still clear because I hadn't had a drop to drink, I remember feeling that the good guy was going to win.

Even if it did take him a while.

Around the same time, I met a guy named Dave, who was a regular churchgoer. One afternoon, as we were finishing up a session in the gym, he asked me if I'd be interested in attending a church service with him. Having never been to a service, I agreed.

Stepping into the church a few days later, I wasn't sure what to expect. The building was plain. The people seemed calm and disinterested. But that all changed as soon as the music started up and the pastor began preaching. I can't say that I retained much of what the guy said, but one memory does stand out. Near the end of the service, everyone in the room but me stuck their hands in the air, praising God and singing along to an unfamiliar hymn. After a minute I decided to join in. Then I turned to Dave and asked him if he wanted to grab breakfast after church.

"What are you doing, man?" he said, whispering.

"What?"

Dave nudged me on the elbow, and I looked around the room. Everyone's hands were down but mine.

"Sorry!" I said, probably with a little more volume than I'd intended.

I tucked my hands back under my legs and listened to the rest of the service. Never once did it occur to me that I would ever set foot in a church again. But God had other plans for me. In the years to come, Dave would become one of my closest friends; he'd also serve as a pastor at Living Hope, where I'd learn he had a beautiful singing voice.

But again, I'm getting ahead of myself.

My final competition as a semiprofessional bodybuilder occurred when I was about nineteen. And it was a big one.

Mr. Teenage Washington was held about three hours north of

my hometown at a convention center in downtown Seattle. Arnold Schwarzenegger, the man who'd inspired me and my friends to pick up weights in the first place, was the judge. I strode onto the stage in another Speedo—this one blue—and posed, excited beyond words that the Big Man was watching me. When he clapped me on the back and told me I did a good job, I felt like I was getting his personal approval. I was elated.

Once again, I went straight from the stage over to Michelle, who by then was officially my girlfriend. On the way out we happened to meet Schwarzenegger, who'd been hanging out in the alley outside the arena. I got together with him, and he congratulated me again. Michelle snapped a picture, which I still have somewhere.

As we got closer, I told Michelle all about my life up until that point: my dad's death, Dean walking out on me, and everything that had happened since. She suggested I might want to think about developing a deeper relationship with God, and I said I'd consider it, barely thinking about what the words even meant.

I think I went to church with her a few times, but I don't remember anything about it. Even as I sang the hymns and recited the prayers along with her pastor, doing it in an extra loud voice so Michelle could hear me, my heart was closed to God. Once, she told me that she couldn't see herself marrying someone who wasn't a Christian, and I asked her where to go to become a Christian. I said a prayer that felt real at the time, although I have realized in the years since that it wasn't. I only wanted to make Michelle happy.

But my heart was being softened, even if I didn't fully realize it at the time.

Michelle satisfied a longing that I'd had my whole life: to know that I mattered, that I was loved, that I was accepted, that I was heard. She checked those boxes.

Over the next few months, we went to church together more often, and I tried like hell to pay attention. Given that I had a serious case of what would now be called ADHD, this wasn't easy.

It also didn't help that the pastor, an older guy, spoke in long sentences that seemed to be drawn from the same script he'd been using for fifty years. I couldn't relate to a single thing he was saying. Back then, I thought church was mostly about telling people what they weren't supposed to do. Don't be mean to people. Don't cheat on your wife. And most importantly, don't skip church.

I was in my late teens, and I never met a person who tried to appeal to *my* life experience. All I got was people telling me rules and letting me know the severe—like, *you'll end up in hell* kind of severe—consequences for not following those rules. And since I've never been a guy who loves rules, I had kind of a block about really getting close to God. I prayed my prayers and I even volunteered at the church for a while, but it was mostly for Michelle. I figured that someday I might get closer to God, but I didn't care whether it happened.

I didn't care about anything other than staying alive, getting stronger, and impressing a dad who'd died when I was four years old.

Looking back, I'm amazed that Michelle agreed to marry me.

But after only a few months of dating, that's exactly what she did.

We were married in a small ceremony at the First Christian Church on Main Street in Vancouver. It was December 26, 1983, probably the worst day of the year to get married. Outside the church doors, a winter storm was ripping through town, covering everything in sheets of ice and blowing out windows in buildings.

But our small crew was happy.

Looking at Michelle in her white dress that day, I felt happiness that I had never believed was possible for me. For the first time in my life, I felt that I didn't need to do anything to earn her love.

But I *wanted* to make myself a better man for her. I wanted to give her everything she'd ever wanted and to make sure she was never unhappy for even a second. We walked out of the church and headed straight for a two-day honeymoon in Newport, Oregon. That first night, I was so happy and relaxed that I fell asleep right on the hotel bed. Michelle tells me she ate ice cream right next to me. The best days of our lives were beginning. The next morning, when I awoke beside my new wife, I could have sworn I heard a voice in the back of my head repeating strange words.

Everything is going to be fine.

Chapter 5

The foot flew at my face in slow motion.

I was standing with my fists at the level of my chest in the garage of my friend Duane, preparing to throw a punch that was supposed to knock out a guy named Garth, who was sparring with me. But I had screwed up the timing, and now a collision was imminent.

My mind went blank.

For the past few years things had been going well. Michelle and I had purchased a small house, and I had served three years in the United States Air Force. We had a four-year-old son named David and a daughter on the way. Despite retaining a little of my youthful exuberance, I had quickly moved up the ranks at McChord Air Force Base, becoming the base commander's executive assistant. There, I had met Duane, who'd introduced me to tae kwon do as a way of channeling my angry impulses into something more constructive. He'd also introduced me to his lovely wife, Trinette, who became fast friends with Michelle. Duane and I had met during a competition at the air force called Below the Zone and become fast friends. Unlike scrapping at parties, tae kwon do had rules. There was a belt system. Sometimes we even wore head gear. My friends and I could get out our aggression on the mats, and no one would ever have to walk away bleeding with only minutes to live.

Or so we thought.

My friend's foot hit me right at the bridge of my nose, where a giant vein called the sphenopalatine artery sits. This artery, which is the main way blood gets from the brain to the rest of the body, severed from the impact. Blood spurted into my eyes and down my face. I could taste it in the back of my throat.

Suddenly I was dizzy. Confused. The world was a series of pictures, and the sound didn't match what I was seeing.

In the back of my mind a scary thought appeared: *You're twenty-five years old. Exactly the age your dad was when he died.* All my life I'd been scared of reaching this age. I didn't know why.

But my friends, including Duane, assured me that I'd just gotten a bloody nose. It was common in combat sports. He apologized half-heartedly for pairing me with Garth, a black belt, when I was only a white belt, and I managed to get home with a towel pressed to my nose.

But the bleeding wouldn't stop.

A few minutes later Michelle walked in with David. To this day he says he remembers walking into the house and seeing blood all over the walls and the floor, along with bloody handprints on almost every surface.

I remember very little other than Michelle taking me to the hospital as the world went fuzzy. After what felt like only a few seconds, we were in a hospital room. I was beginning to black out. Doctors gave me shots and began prepping me for surgery. I looked down at my body and saw more blood than I'd ever seen before.

My own blood, I thought, thinking of Uncle Jim. *Not good.*

I was pretty much out for most of what followed. I'm told that in those early hours, my face looked like someone had whacked me with a sack full of hammers. My nose was swollen. I was pale from blood loss. After about an hour of surgeons working on me, I'm told that a doctor took Michelle aside and prepared her for the possibility that I might not make it.

"If he has a priest, I would call him," the doctor told Michelle.

If I'd been awake, I might have objected to this. The last thing

I would have wanted to see before dying—if that's what had to happen to me—was the boring, judgmental face of my pastor. Luckily Michelle called Neal Curtiss, the pastor at a church we'd been to once or twice at that point, and he answered the call. Around two o'clock in the morning this man I barely knew walked into my hospital room and began praying over me.

I don't remember waking up for the first time. What I do remember is a clear voice in my head—the same one I'd heard on my wedding day—telling me to be grateful I survived, then asking a question.

What happens after this?

At the time, I still believed I was probably going to die. So did the doctors. I looked to the foot of the bed and saw David, my four-year-old son, who would never see his daddy again. I pictured him growing up, as I had, without a father—bitter and angry at his life and God. I desperately wished for a second chance, an opportunity to do things differently.

In the end, I got one.

My strength came back. My eyes opened. The swelling began draining from my nose, and the doctors began unhooking me from all the machines that had been keeping me alive.

But no matter how many times I tried to feel happy that I'd pulled through, hugging my son and kissing Michelle and laughing with my tae kwon do partner about how close he'd almost come to killing me, I couldn't do it.

That question kept nagging at me.

What happens after this?

Religious conversions are strange.

During my years studying the Bible, I've read accounts of hundreds of them. The most famous one, which we all learn about in Sunday school, is Paul's. One day he was persecuting Christians as Saul, and the next day he was on his butt in the road, staring up at a bright white light that told him to believe in Christ.

I don't know much about shining white lights. I've never seen one. But I do remember the suddenness with which God spoke to me for the first time. I understand the fear that Paul must have felt upon seeing the angel who told him about Christ. I know what it's like to have an awareness of the world that simply wasn't there a second ago, and to feel like you need to reorient your whole life to accommodate this new awareness.

I didn't come out of the hospital a Christian. Not really. I did have a new interest in attending church, though, and this time around I was going to listen. Luckily Pastor Neal was far more engaging than some of the other pastors Michelle and I had endured over the years. He had a sharp, accessible style that even my ADHD-addled brain could follow.

After a few weeks I joined a small group led by Pastor Neal. Together we read the Bible closely, and we tried to apply it to our lives. One night, during a quiet moment in the small group, Pastor Neal looked straight at me and asked, "If you died right now, do you think you'd go to heaven?"

Coming from him, who'd seen the fear in my eyes firsthand when I was on my deathbed—or what I *thought* was my death-bed—it was an intense question.

Without hesitating I said no.

I knew the truth in my soul, and I wanted things to be different.

So on that day—October 4, 1988—I asked Christ into my heart.

But it was more than an empty prayer this time. As I cried out to God to save me, I sensed an insatiable desire to walk with Jesus, to follow Him, and to surrender my life to Him.

Neal put his hands on my shoulders and prayed over me. So did everyone in my small group.

I had never felt more accepted in my life.

Over the next few years I worked hard to finish my undergraduate degree. For a while I'd been planning to go to law school. But my experience with God had changed those plans. Now I was going to attend seminary and become a pastor.

One day after church I walked into Neal Curtiss's office and told him my plans. He was thrilled. When I asked if there was a way I could get involved immediately, he suggested volunteering.

"You're good with young people," he said. "Why don't you try speaking with our youth group?"

I thought about it. I had always liked kids, and by this point I had two of my own—David and a daughter named Katie, who'd been born at the same hospital I went to when I got my nose kicked in. I figured preaching to kids would be worth a shot. One night that week I headed to the church in my street clothes and met with the handful of kids who made up the church youth group. We talked about our lives, our problems, and the things that made us feel far from God. I was surprised to find that the more I told them about *my* life, the more they seemed to trust me. Unlike most authority figures they'd met up to that point, I didn't try to pretend I had all the answers. I was willing to get down on their level—which was pretty much where I lived anyway—and talk about real life. Because I was willing to do that, these kids felt comfortable telling me things they probably hadn't ever told adults before.

After a while my entrepreneurial spirit kicked in. If I was going to reach kids, I wanted to reach all of them. Everywhere I went, I saw kids who'd grown up in circumstances similar to my own. They were lonely, confused, and going through life without a purpose. I couldn't count on every single one of them getting kicked in the face the way I did to make a spiritual conversion happen. I decided to meet them where they were.

At first I went to the smoking areas outside high schools.

I'd talk with the kids for a while about what was going on with them, and then I'd let them know I ran a youth group out of Vancouver Community Church on Wednesday nights. The first time I tried it, I got a few kids for the first meeting. We ate pizza and talked about the problems that kids in my neighborhood tended to face: absent parents, poverty, lack of direction. The next week, it was a few dozen kids. I was genuinely shocked at how quickly these kids accepted God into their hearts. I was amazed by their dedication to God's Word and how closely they examined the Bible passages we were reading.

Within a few months the youth group at Vancouver Community was extremely large for the size of the church. We began meeting several times a week, reading from the Bible and trying to apply those passages to our lives. I never had to work hard to steer the conversation toward God and Christian principles. The kids did that all by themselves. When they had problems, they'd come to me, and I'd help them work through whatever they were dealing with. I would do this despite the fact that I still had quite a bit in my own life that I hadn't figured out. Michelle always came with me, and we spoke with the kids together.

I still dealt with anger issues. It was in my blood. No matter how hard I tried to calm down, I still couldn't stand bullies. Once, I was sitting in a restaurant with Michelle, and I heard a guy at the next table screaming at his wife. *Really* screaming, like they were the only two people in the room. He called her all kinds of words that I don't feel comfortable reprinting here. So I walked over and threw my napkin in his food. I asked him if he wanted to go outside to the parking lot and settle it, and he backed down. I didn't enjoy doing things like this because I thought it made me look tough. There was something about seeing people who couldn't help themselves getting picked on that made me feel I needed to step in.

It wasn't the best way to deal with my issues. But it was the only way I had. Rather than hating myself, I turned to the Bible, which happened to be full of imperfect people who managed to please God with their actions on earth. I read about David, who despite his flaws and mistakes was still considered a man after God's own heart. I read about Peter, who denied Jesus three times yet became a foundational leader in the early church.

If they could do it, so could I.

A few months into my tenure as the youth pastor at Vancouver Community, Neal decided it was time for me to get up and preach in front of everyone—or, at the very least, to tell my story to the world and see what they thought.

Chapter 6

My hands shook. I had to grip the podium to make them stop. In the audience a sea of about a hundred faces stared back at me. We were gathered at Burnside Shelter in downtown Portland, a shelter for homeless people that offered religious services and food on weekday afternoons.

I had a stack of papers in front of me, all covered in the small font I'd used to type out my sermon. On these pages was a long, detailed dissertation on a passage from Luke 12. The passage, which I had copied on the top of the paper, told the parable of the rich fool.

I read the whole thing, word for word:

> "The ground of a certain rich man yielded an abundant harvest. He thought to himself, 'What shall I do? I have no place to store my crops.' Then he said, 'This is what I'll do. I will tear down my barns and build bigger ones, and there I will store my surplus grain. And I'll say to myself, "You have plenty of grain laid up for many years. Take life easy; eat, drink and be merry."' But God said to him, 'You fool! This very night your life will be demanded from you. Then who will get what you have prepared for yourself?' This is how it will be with whoever stores up things for themselves but is not rich toward God." (vv. 16–21)

In my eyes I had been the rich fool, chasing earthly pleasures, focused only on fulfilling my desires and storing away stuff. I'd been saved by the thought that someday my life would be required of me.

As far as I was concerned, my one job was to make people see God the way that I did: as an all-knowing, all-loving presence in the world who could bring happiness and salvation to anyone, no matter where they've been or what they've done.

I began with a few off-script remarks, then launched into what I'd written. Right away I knew I was talking too fast.

But I couldn't stop.

I blew right through the passage, then offered a few more off-the-cuff thoughts about God. Out in the crowd I saw smiles and wide eyes. People were liking it. Liking *me*. They thought I was good at this. I loved the feeling. At the very least, it was nice to be getting some attention for something other than beating people up or having giant muscles. When I said the last words of my sermon—which encouraged everyone to accept Christ into their hearts as I had done—everyone in the crowd got to their feet and applauded.

I was beaming.

Afterward I walked over to the director of Burnside, who'd been working in his office while I spoke.

"I think it went pretty well," I said.

"Great."

"Do they usually clap like that?"

He looked up from his desk and said, "No. They don't."

"Wow."

"Wow is right."

"So . . . I guess something I said must have really connected, right? I mean, they seemed really pumped up out there."

The director laughed.

"What?"

"How long were you supposed to speak?"

"Thirty-five minutes," I said.

The director pointed at the clock with his pen. "You were up there for five and a half minutes," he said. "They were clapping because they got to eat a half hour early."

I looked toward the back of the room, where single-file lines had begun forming in front of long metal tables. The cafeteria workers were scrambling to get everything ready, fastening their hairnets and calling people in from their smoke breaks.

I was a little embarrassed. But not enough to make me forget the way all those people had looked up at me as I spoke. I knew I had reached people.

In the weeks to come, I returned to Burnside a few times, and I got to talking with some of the homeless people there. More than a few said that my words had affected them.

Speaking to these people, I came to understand three things. First, I knew that I was a hopeless sinner who would have spent eternity in hell if God hadn't intervened. Second, I knew that while I was living blindly in my sin, Christ died for me. While I was making fun of Christians and looking down on the church, Christ was right there pursuing me. Third, I knew that I could do nothing else with my life now but give it up to serve the God who had pursued me. I knew that there were thousands of people just like me who still needed to know the truth about God and experience His love.

God was calling me to seek the lost, and He was calling me to serve His church.

After seeing me do so well with the youth group, Pastor Neal gave me a little more responsibility at Vancouver Community. I would often stand up at the altar with him during Sunday services. I also helped out on the business side, drawing on some of my experience running a janitorial business and trying to apply those lessons to our church.

One day he asked if I would be willing to fill in on a more permanent basis.

"It's been years since I've taken even one day off," he told me. "And I'd like to take a vacation. Would you mind running things for a bit while I'm gone?"

I said I would, happy to have the new responsibility.

And I ran with it.

A few days into Neal's vacation, I heard about a building across the road that was up for sale. It was giant, and it seemed perfect for our growing ministry. Even as the general congregation held steady at just under a hundred people, the youth group—which was my purview—had ballooned to about seventy-five kids, and it was growing every day. A new building, I figured, would give us tons of space to hold events and workshops. It would give troubled kids a place to go other than the streets.

I called the guy selling the building, and we negotiated a deal relatively quickly. I was surprised by how much I enjoyed the process. Within a few days we had paperwork all "in pencil," as they say, waiting on Neal's desk. When he returned a few days later, he picked up the document and asked what it was.

I explained what I'd done and how I thought the deal could be structured using the cash we had on hand and a small loan that used our current real estate holdings as collateral. Neal seemed impressed.

"Let's do it," he said.

And just like that, we were moving into a new building, and I had a front-row seat to the reconstruction of Vancouver Community from the ground up. In my head I took notes on how to arrange a room, coordinate volunteers, and spread the gospel in a way that was effective. After the move, membership ballooned even further. By the time we were fully moved in, our youth group was bigger than those of churches that were ten times our size. Michelle was especially good at helping me connect with the kids. Together, we could tackle any issue they had, and we'd always do it by referencing the Word of God.

Something big was happening, and I was happy to be a part of it.

In 1995 David turned eleven years old. Standing beside him as he blew out the candles on his cake, I couldn't help but think about how I'd felt on my own birthdays growing up, wandering around the house missing my dad. I felt blessed to still be around for my family. By this point, our daughter Katie was seven, and we'd welcomed another daughter, Hannah, in 1994.

Something in my heart told me it was time for a change.

Over the next few months I read the Bible cover to cover. When I was done, I read it again. Every week I would attend small group meetings and dissect verses, trying to understand the original contexts in which they were written. In time, my Bible began to look like the beat-up one Michelle had pulled out during the party when we were teenagers. I finally understood the impulse that had driven her to walk out to her car and get the Bible during that time of extreme stress. Every time I opened my Bible, I found something new. The Word of God brought me comfort unlike anything I had ever known.

One night, reading through the New Testament, I came across this passage in 2 Corinthians 4:18: "We don't look at the troubles we can see now; rather, we fix our gaze on things that cannot be seen. For the things we see now will soon be gone, but the things we cannot see will last forever" (NLT).

I thought about the meaning of the words for a long time. During my next session with my small group, I brought it up with a few friends. A few hours later we'd resolved to start an evangelistic ministry called Focus One. The group's name took inspiration from the verse in 2 Corinthians: We were going to reach out and convert people to Christianity, focusing on the unseen.

Right away we sent letters to each of the four hundred churches in our county, letting them know about our ministry and our amazing plan to reach the world for Christ. Then we manned the phones, waiting for the calls to come in.

We waited.

And then waited some more.

But not one invitation came. The phone lines in our small makeshift office were quiet. As the weeks wore on, we walked around the church in a dejected state. One afternoon Pastor Neal noticed. He asked us if we'd do a three-night crusade over Easter weekend there at Vancouver Community Church. I was ecstatic and thankful. Clearly he was doing us a favor by allowing our small group to take over the church during the most important three-day stretch of the year. I returned to the message from Luke 12 that I'd delivered at the homeless shelter, polishing it and adding passages that I thought would inspire people to dedicate their lives to Christ.

My goal was to baptize at least one person—to make someone in the crowd open their eyes to God the way I had done as Pastor Neal prayed over me in the hospital. To do that, I'd need to connect. I'd also need to speak slowly.

I practiced almost every night in front of Michelle, who was supportive and loving every step of the way. Years earlier, she'd told me about a dream she'd had as a little girl—one in which she stood in front of an old country church amid waves of grain, holding hands with her husband, who was a pastor. Now it seemed that the dream was coming true. While I practiced, David ran around the living room, listening to me rehearse, with Katie close behind him. Watching David laughing and jumping into Michelle's arms, I couldn't help but think of how different his childhood was from my own. Unlike me, David and Katie were going to have two loving parents. No one was going to lay a hand on them. I knew that he would be able to avoid all the traps I'd fallen into during my troubled adolescence.

But I was wrong, at least when it came to David.

The final night of Easter weekend arrived.

I put on my best suit and headed to church, where a few members of my family showed up to support me. Even Uncle Jim, who hadn't exactly set me on the path to becoming a pastor, pulled on a pair of khakis and took a seat in the back.

For the past few days I'd been preaching like crazy. I felt like I finally had a handle on my speaking voice. My palms were no longer sweating. By the second service, I was able to get through the whole message without my voice warbling or my body shaking.

On the last night I stood up and asked if anyone was ready to surrender their life to Christ. I shared the teaching from Luke 12 again, reciting the story mostly from memory. I said that I would likely have heard the same words from God (*"You fool!"*) if I hadn't been kicked in the face and spared by God's grace.

I gave the altar call. Music began to play behind me.

For a while no one came up.

Great, I thought. *It's like the phones all over again.*

Then, from a few hundred feet away, I saw an old man in a suit come walking up the aisle.

Pop.

At first I didn't believe it was him. I didn't even know he was there. I had no words. This was a man who had lived as I had, far from God, and here he was in front of me—the man who had sacrificed so much of his own life to raise me—about to receive eternal life.

As he came forward, we embraced. Pop began to cry.

"Pop, you're going to receive Christ!" I told him, almost crying myself.

I thought of all the days Pop had spent driving me around town. All the times he'd picked me up from the police station when I'd broken the law yet again. Now, finally, I had become something he could be proud of. I had led him to Christ. At the moment it felt like the least I could have done for him.

As we embraced, God put a vision in my heart. I saw a church that would spread all over the globe, ministering to people just like my grandfather. I wanted to reach people who had never been to church in their lives and who lived far outside the light of the Lord just like I had until I was in my midtwenties. All around the world there were thousands of people waiting to be saved.

And for the first time, I felt like it was my job to save them.

Part 2

CATASTROPHIC GROWTH

Chapter 7

For most people, opening a church is a bad idea.

It doesn't matter how charismatic you are as a preacher or how many people tell you that you've inspired them and you need to set up your own shop. Most churches fail within five years, and the ones that make it longer than that usually sputter along with fewer than a hundred members.

I knew that the odds of success were low, but I didn't care. When I did something, I was all in. God was calling me, and I had spent too long ignoring His voice.

Besides, I was no stranger to bad ideas. Compared to whacking yourself on the head with an A&W mug or shooting up off-label steroids in pursuit of a few extra pounds of muscle, embarking on a risky business venture was nothing.

So that was that: I was going to open my own church.

One of the first things I did was call Neal Curtiss, the man who'd led me to Christ and taught me important lessons about how to minister to people. "It's important to me that I have your blessing," I said.

He was shocked.

Over the years Neal and I had grown close. He had been especially kind to Michelle, who'd brought me in from the cold and put me on the path to connect with God. At first I thought his resistance to me starting my own church was paternal—the kind of thing a father feels for a son when he's about to leave for college. Toward the end of the call, though, his voice took on a harder edge.

"Fine," he said. "But I don't want you operating anywhere around Vancouver. You have to be out of the city."

I was surprised, but I agreed.

At the time, Michelle and I were living in a modest home at the base of Mount St. Helens, in a town called Yacolt. It was about forty minutes outside of Vancouver. We had a few friends over, including Duane and Trinette, and began talking about what starting a church might look like. Over the years, Duane and Trinette had become our best friends; we'd moved to Vancouver with them after Duane and I got out of the air force. Duane went to seminary and got a master of divinity degree, which was more academic, and I got my master of arts. Once we had our degrees, Duane was the first person to tell me that if I wanted to start a church, he would help me. Sitting around the table that day, we determined that the first thing we'd need was a building, and because of Neal's reluctance to have me strike out on my own, that building couldn't be in Vancouver.

About nine months later, I pulled up to a squat building called Manor Grange on a main street in Battle Ground, Washington. Originally, it was built for farmers who wanted to take a break from their isolated lives and come into town for bingo, dancing, and other social events. Inside, it looked like a rummage sale. In the middle of the large hall, I saw an old man sweeping the floor and collecting scattered debris. I walked up to him and introduced myself. He said his name was Mel and that he was the caretaker.

"I'm sweeping up after a church," he said. "They just left. It was their last service."

"Wow," I told him, taking it as a kind of sign. "That's *great*. I'm actually looking to rent some space here myself."

Mel let out a hard chuckle.

"It's actually *not* great. I hate churches. They never have any money, and they always leave the place a mess. Anyway, what were you looking to rent the place for. A wedding?"

"No . . . ," I said. "I was actually thinking about something different. Something more permanent."

"Yeah? What?"

I cringed a little and said, "A church?"

I thought he was going to throw his broom at me.

"No," he said. "Absolutely not. No way. Do you see what I'm dealing with here? These churches, they never last, and they never have any money. And they just . . ."

It went on like that for a while. As Mel hurled complaints at me about the past few churches he'd allowed into the grange, I helped him sweep up the room and organize the folding chairs that the last congregation had left behind. By the time we were done, I had worn him down. He agreed to rent the building to me and my new church for $400 a month—which, at the time, was a lot of money for me.

I also made him a promise: "If this place is not better in every way six months from now, we'll move out and you'll never see us again."

Over the next week, Michelle and I worked with Duane and Trinette to get the place ready. We hung a sign above the door that read Living Hope, and we spread the word that there was a new church in town.

About thirty people attended our first service. I stood at the front of the room in a suit jacket and tie and khakis, trying to look like a grown-up so that people would respect me. I had no idea what I was doing. But I believed that if I wanted to succeed, I needed to dress like my heroes. At the time, that meant men such as the Reverend Billy Graham. For years I had been watching these men—especially Billy Graham—minister to people with a fervor that made me want to do the same thing. Reverend Graham's dedication to Christ was inspiring, and so was the high-minded, florid language he used to speak about God. Listening to the man preach made me feel like I was listening to the gospel being beamed right down from heaven.

But I soon learned that I wasn't Billy Graham. I hadn't grown up on a farm around folksy Southern people. I was from Vancouver, Washington, and so were the people I was ministering to.

As such, I needed to keep my voice authentic.

I still remember the day it hit me. I was pacing up and down in front of the congregation at the grange, dressed in my shirt and tie, doing my best impression of Reverend Graham. By then we'd grown to about sixty people. I was pointing to my Bible and offering an interpretation of Scripture filled with data points and quotes from secondary sources. I was trying to be a shining example that my parishioners could aspire to.

In other words, I wasn't being myself.

I was learning, with the same people I was leading, how to live a life that honors God. Other than following Jesus, I didn't know a single thing about how to live a good life. Sure, I had made some good decisions. I'd had the good sense to marry Michelle, for one thing, and to listen when she told me what to do. We'd had three beautiful children, and we'd managed to beat the odds by opening a successful church together. But other than that, my life was just a long series of screw-ups and flailing attempts to get by. I'd beaten people up. I'd done stupid things as a kid. I must have had some nerve to get up and tell other people how to live when I was ten times more screwed up than any of them.

Instead of taking off my tie, throwing it onto the wooden floor, and walking out, I decided to tell them all about it.

"I know what it's like to be broken," I said, veering off the track of whatever sermon I was in the middle of. "My dad died when I was four years old. He ran his car into a tree, and the cops found twenty-five beer cans on the floor of his car. He was supposed to have me with him, so thank God he didn't."

The faces of everyone in the crowd perked up.

"I had a stepfather who beat my mother and me. I wanted to kill him, but I couldn't. When I was old enough, I started getting in fights. *Lots* of fights. Beating up kids on the block if they looked at me wrong. My uncles noticed, and they started throwing me into the ring with kids from around the neighborhood, making us take our shirts off and beat the crap out of each other."

I looked around, wondering if anyone would care that I'd said *crap* in a church.

No one did.

"I usually won. From then on, I got in fights all the time, pummeling kids to prove I was tough like my dad. It took me years to realize that I was—and I still *am*—just a four-year-old kid trying to impress a daddy who's dead."

And on, and on, and on.

By the end of my speech—which I did manage to steer back to the text for that sermon—the room was dead quiet. A chair squeaked. A few heavy smokers in the back let out coughs. I led the group in prayer, and I felt the Holy Spirit fill up the room. I think everyone did. If the Kool-Aid Man had come crashing through the grange that night with suitcases full of money in his hands, not a single person at Living Hope would have looked up. Standing before my small congregation, I felt like I was standing squarely in the blessability zone, doing the work that God had put me on earth to do.

Still, that old voice was in the back of my head.

More, it said. *Get more.*

Only now, instead of one more rep on the squat rack, it was one more soul for Christ.

From that day on, I preached without a tie.

I wanted to reach the people I'd grown up around. And the

people I'd grown up around were more likely to strangle someone with a tie than they were to wear one. Guys like Uncle Jim and my dad didn't want to hear some college-educated preacher get up and present his polished, paint-by-numbers account of how to live according to the gospel. They wanted to hear real stuff from a person who'd been through some of the same things they had.

In Vancouver, Washington, in the late 1990s, that meant unemployment. It meant addiction and domestic abuse and a kind of hopelessness about the future. Behind the small-town facade, people were truly hurting. Peel back the shiny exterior of *any* small town in America, and I believe you'll find people who are lost and suffering, waiting for someone to speak to them.

All that time, I was extremely careful to be respectful to Neal Curtiss. I made sure to tell anyone who came to services that we weren't interested in poaching members from other congregations. We wanted to be a church for people like me and my grandfather, who would never have gone to church otherwise.

In Vancouver, churches had popped up occasionally. Most coasted along for a few years, never attracting more than a hundred or so members. Church-planting organizations such as the North American Mission Board had tried repeatedly to break into the Pacific Northwest with no luck. At the time we started Living Hope in my house, my home city was smack in the middle of the least churched part of the United States. According to a survey taken at the time, just over 30 percent of people regularly attended services. Even fewer than that said they believed in God at all.

I understood why Mel, our landlord, had gotten frustrated. Every time a church popped up in town, it would last for a few months and then go belly-up. I don't know how long it took for him to realize that Living Hope—which, much to our surprise, was adding new members every week—would be different. It was probably the fifth or sixth time I drove to his house and dropped off the $100 check I gave him once a week. Maybe it was the time he walked through the building and saw Duane and a bunch of volunteers fixing problems with the plumbing and electrical systems, putting their blue-collar knowledge to good use for us and everyone else who used the building. All I know is that three years later, when we had grown to 140 people, Mel was a friend.

But the swelling congregation left me with a decision to make. The building, which had been a good home for our young church, could no longer sustain us. The portion where we held the kids' ministry would flood in the winter, and we would find ourselves down in the basement trying to vacuum the water out. In the summer I would sweat from the stifling heat caused by packing hundreds of people—our congregants and their guests—into such a small location. It was time for a change.

Before long we found an auditorium at Prairie High School that had rented to churches before. The space was huge, and it had a stage. I figured it was good enough, and we made the move from the grange to the high school. Our congregation grew immensely as soon as we hit the new building. I don't know whether it was the ease of the commute or the new space, but people loved it.

A few months after the move, I sat down with my elders and asked what we could do to bring even more people in.

"We will do anything short of sin to reach one person for Jesus Christ," I said.

We brainstormed, then took the ideas and ran with them. It didn't take long for our weekly planning meetings to become all-out competitions to see who could come up with the most unique idea for the next Sunday's service.

One Sunday morning, we did a service based on the popular kids' movie *Monsters, Inc.* Our wonderful staff and our volunteers designed a full set. Something about the performance aspect appealed to me. I could feel that people were listening more closely than they would otherwise. I soon realized that many of the people who were coming to these services had grown up in strict religious traditions. Church, to them, was boring. In some traditions it was forbidden even to put up pictures of the Easter Bunny; all the glory was supposed to go to Jesus Christ, and kitschy holiday items could have no part in that.

I saw things differently. I didn't think there was any contradiction between having fun and giving glory to God. Anything that was going to bring in more people off the street was okay with me. Our volunteers agreed. For our first Easter at the high school, we set up an "amazing egg maze" for the kids that took them all over the property. In my mind, we weren't competing with the church down the street. We were competing with Sunday afternoon football games and the comfort of a warm bed. Anything we could do to get people in the doors, and get them excited, was okay with me.

But it wasn't enough.

Around that time I learned that 90 percent of churches that offer only one weekly service never grow. So we added a second service at nine o'clock. When it was over, people would stick around, talking to Michelle and me about how nice it was to have a place they could come to for a sense of community. Sometimes I would hang out in the back, leaning against the wall with a hot dog and watching people come together. Housewives made friends with day laborers; kids from radically different backgrounds ran around playing games amid the folding chairs—all because some guy had kicked me in the face and set me on a journey to find Christ.

It was a good feeling. For once, I was entertaining people in a way that didn't involve getting repeatedly punched in the head. And I was leading them to a better life in Christ while I was at it. Most importantly, I wasn't taking a dime for salary. Duane, whom I still consider one of my best friends, made sure there were firewalls between me and the money to avoid any illusions of impropriety. I was still working with my partners on our janitorial cleaning business, taking care of about three million square feet of tile flooring a day, and that brought in more than enough money.

The church was something I did purely for the mission, and the mission was going well.

A few years later our membership numbers had swelled again. Every weekend, we'd have bigger and bigger groups show up for worship. Even I was amazed by the speed at which we'd grown. The elders, by then a close-knit group that included many excellent volunteers we'd met over the years, began talking about acquiring our own building.

Luckily, I had one in mind.

Chapter 8

Over the years, I'd driven past Prairie Community Church hundreds of times. It was housed in a giant building less than a mile from Neal Curtiss's church. The building itself was magnificent: all new carpets and spotless comfortable chairs, along with a few large rooms for youth group meetings and other activities. It sat on fifteen acres. Walking through it, I figured it could hold at least a thousand people.

Of course, I didn't know for sure.

At the time, Prairie Community was struggling. The number of full-time members had fallen below fifty people, and no one knew how to bring it back up. Most Sundays, the pastor ministered to a group that could have fit in my living room back in Yacolt. One day, I called the youth pastor and asked if we could meet. Over lunch he told me that things were even worse than they looked from the outside. The church owed about $800,000 to the bank, and they were burning cash trying to attract new members.

I asked for a meeting with the church staff, and a few days later I was sitting in a shiny conference room on the first floor of the building with the elders from Living Hope, waiting for the Prairie Community team to roll in. They arrived, taking their seats one by one, and asked me what I was thinking.

"It's simple," I said. "You have a building, and we have people. I suggest merging."

There were nods and murmurs of agreement. A few of their elders asked questions, and I answered them to the best of my ability. After several minutes it looked like we were all set to move forward.

Then a man at the end of the table spoke up, asking questions that had a sharp edge to them. For the first time in a while, I felt my fighter's instinct kick in, wanting to walk over and square up to the guy. Which, I know now, probably would have gone horribly for me.

The man's name was Ron Webb, and he was about six foot five. Although he wasn't yet an elder of the church, he was definitely the alpha male of the group. When he spoke, everyone listened. If he didn't like an idea, no one did.

Before I could answer a single one of his questions, Ron was pounding his fists on the table, telling me what a stupid idea it was to merge our churches. He believed I was trying to take advantage of them in their moment of need. He believed I was a joke and a charlatan, more interested in advancing my own agenda than leading people to Christ. He called me names that probably hadn't ever been uttered in a church before, screaming most of them like a guy who wasn't used to not getting his own way.

"I mean, what are we *doing* here?" he said. "You should all be ashamed of yourselves. We are *not* allowing a takeover of this church."

Then I felt a calming presence, and my hands relaxed. My whole *body* relaxed. I leaned back in my chair and waited for Ron to finish. When he was done, I said, "I don't think this is what God wants here. So I want to say thank you, and we're not going to pursue this option."

We all stood to leave.

I was halfway out the door when I heard Ron call out to me.

"Wait," he said. "Sit back down."

I turned around and looked at Ron, who'd come slightly out of his chair. His countenance had changed completely. There was a kindness in his face that hadn't been there a few seconds earlier. He wasn't exactly ready to wrap me in a big hug, but he seemed willing to work with me.

Which was exactly what he did.

We hammered out the finer points of a merger, and everyone seemed happy. As we were about to wrap up, Ron leaned back in his chair, arms folded. He looked around the room and said, "So when do we want to try this?"

I said I was game for anything.

"How about this Sunday?"

It wasn't until we were outside, flying high from how well the meeting had gone, that I remembered it was Thursday afternoon. So we began reaching out, letting everyone know that we had a new building for services. The response was overwhelming. Watching the people file in, I knew that we had something special.

We were home.

After our first service at the church, I walked into the office of a founding pastor, an older guy named Don Coonrod, who had overseen construction of the building.

"You know, John," he said, looking around wistfully. "I've always had a dream about this place. I've never told anyone about it."

"What was it?"

"It's stupid, really. But I always imagined that someday, I'd be able to get a thousand people into this building. While they were building it, I thought that'd be the dream. *A thousand* people, all praying together and worshiping. I was starting to think it wasn't possible."

My heart fluttered as I realized where he was going with this.

"This morning, I had someone at the door counting people as they came in. When the service was over, they told me exactly how many people you preached to today."

"You're not telling me it was a thousand," I said, barely able to comprehend the number.

The pastor smiled.

"It was one thousand and one."

A few months into our time at the new building, I had one of the most amazing experiences of my life. At this time I was still running the janitorial business, overseeing hundreds of employees who cleaned millions of square feet of retail space all over the state. The benefits were good, and the work was genuinely enjoyable most of the time. I had a feeling that soon I would need to give up the full-time job and become a pastor. But I wasn't ready to do it yet.

Still, every week brought new signals that this church thing was probably going to become more than a part-time occupation for me. It was my destiny. One week we planned a baptism service. By the night before it was supposed to happen, the list of people who wanted to get baptized was sixty names long, and it included people of all ages. One of my elders was beaming when he came into my office to deliver the news. "It's going to be great," he said. "We're going to perform sixty baptisms! That'll get everyone pumped up."

"That's great news, man," I said.

"Praise God!"

"Praise God is right. Just leave the list on my desk, and I'll go over it, so I know when to call everyone's names."

He checked his pockets, and the color drained from his face.

"Hold on," he said. "I'll be right back. Just hold on."

Ten minutes later I walked outside and found him on his hands and knees, checking under desks for the list of names. Our volunteers were still hitting the phones hard, asking people whether they had Sunday morning plans. Paper rustled in the background. Landlines rang out.

The pastor stood up.

"I lost it."

"That's fine," I said. "Just print out another copy."

He winced.

"You didn't put it in the computer?"

"No."

Again I braced for anger. But it never came. List or no list, we had sixty people who were looking forward to being baptized, and somehow I knew God would find a way to make it happen. I patted the pastor on the shoulder and told him everything was going to be fine. Then I walked into my office, sat down at my desk, and spoke directly to God, as I often did back in those days.

Alright, I said. *This is Your show now, God. There are sixty people out there waiting to be baptized, and I don't know who they are. But You're the God of creation. You're the God who made these people. And I need help.*

It wasn't more than a few seconds before God answered me, speaking in a voice as clear as that of any human being I've ever heard.

Get in the water in your clothes, He said.

And I knew exactly what to do.

Sunday morning, I stood at the front door of the Prairie Community Church building in jeans and a long-sleeve shirt, watching crowds of people come in. The temperature had fallen just below thirty degrees. Behind me I listened as the elders tested the water in the baptismal pool to make sure it was warm.

I said hello to everyone as they rolled in, speaking for a few minutes with anyone I recognized. I tried to tell them how grateful I was that they'd made the trip. Before I knew it, I was up there in the middle of my sermon, staring out at a sea of unfamiliar faces. The church was full. People were standing in the back because they hadn't been able to get seats on the chairs. I paused, stepped forward, and began the call to baptism, trusting that God would take me where I needed to go.

Moving through the packed church, I had the feeling that I was in dangerous territory. I could easily fail. But I had read enough of my Bible to know that dangerous territory is where God sends you when He's got great things in store. He sent Peter to the home of Cornelius, a Gentile, in the book of Acts, breaking the barriers of Jewish exclusivity and spreading the gospel to the Gentiles. He sent Jonah to Nineveh, a city known for its wickedness, to deliver a message of repentance (although that journey wasn't a whole lot of fun for Jonah, who spent a great deal of it in the belly of a whale).

The crowd hushed as my feet hit the water. I hadn't even bothered to remove my shoes. I waded in, shivering in the air-conditioned atmosphere of the church, and invited anyone who felt called to dedicate his or her life to Christ to come up and join me.

The first person was a woman I recognized. I said a prayer over her, laid my hand on her forehead, and laid her back into the water. A small group of guys came up next. Before long, there was a line stretching up the center aisle. I continued praying and preaching as I helped people into the pool, splashing water all over the church, listening to the music from the band and feeling grateful to be exactly where I was.

I stayed in the cold water until every last person who wanted to be baptized was guided into the water and prayed over. For a while I'd counted. But I'd lost track somewhere around a hundred, surrendering to the Holy Spirit and the magic of the morning.

From then on, I decided not to worry.

When something felt right, I would do it. In that building in my hometown of Vancouver, which happened to be a stone's throw from the place I had nervously preached my first halting attempts at sermons, my team and I put on shows that rivaled the best of what Las Vegas had to offer.

One day, in the lead-up to a sermon on Noah's ark, I had the idea to bring live animals to a service. Come Sunday morning, I was watching a live hawk fly all over the room, trying to keep my focus as it made giant circles above the heads of the crowd.

The animal trainer I'd hired also had a giant Bengal tiger named Sundar and one of the monkeys that had been featured in *Pirates of the Caribbean*. Although this man had told me repeatedly not to touch the tiger, I found that I couldn't resist. Just before my closing message of the seventh and final service of the weekend, I stuck my hand out, and then *bam*. This thing reared up and came at me. I thought I was going to die. To this day, there's a video of me on YouTube backing up, taking a moment to contemplate my own mortality, and then asking the congregation to begin our closing prayer. Zoom in close, and you'll be able to see that I peed my pants a little.

For between six and eight weeks at a time, we would put on series that applied directly to people's lives. Many of them included elaborate sets. We brought in giant truckloads of sand for a series on Jonah and rented a giant Cessna plane for a service based on the hit television show *Lost*. For one stretch of about six weeks, I covered the church in razor wire and preached a service based on the show *Prison Break*. A series on the theme "Dangerous Church" involved transforming the building into the Roman Coliseum. My daughter Katie led a kids' music ministry called the "Big Red Bus," and they traveled to different churches in an actual big red bus. Almost every week, there were more people, all with wide eyes and expectant faces, wanting to see what I'd throw at them next.

And we weren't going to let up.

As always, the motto was bigger, faster, leaner.

More, more, more.

Chapter 9

From the moment I saw the four elders from Vancouver Community Church sitting in the back row of chairs, I had a bad feeling.

For a moment I wondered whether they'd come to remind me about the promise I'd made to Neal Curtiss about not coming back to Vancouver. But I didn't think it was likely. My family had remained friendly with Neal over the years, and he'd always seemed proud of my success. In the end, we had the same Boss, and that Boss had written some pretty ironclad rules (one in particular) about being covetous of thy neighbor.

I finished my sermon, keeping one eye on the guys in the back. When the service was over and everyone else had filed out, the four men from Neal's church were still there. I asked what they wanted, and they told me they'd been following the progress of Living Hope. Their church was struggling, and they wanted to know if I could help.

A few minutes later we were sitting in my office. The four elders took chairs on the far side of the room, and I sat at my desk with a few of my pastors beside me. We made our introductions, and then the guys from Vancouver Community got straight to the point. One of the elders proposed financial terms. I nodded along. But something felt wrong. Finally, I blurted out the question that had been nagging at me since I spotted them at the back of the room.

"Where's Neal?"

The faces in the room fell. One of the guys in the corner spoke up and said, "He had a personal problem, and he came to us with it a few months ago and asked us for help."

I thought for a moment. The man who'd brought me to Christ, and who'd been such a good friend to my wife, didn't seem like the kind of guy who'd allow any personal issues that would spiral out of control. But we all harbor secrets. If anything, I thought it was brave of Neal to come forward and admit he had a problem.

"Did you get him help?" I asked.

No one wanted to answer.

So I repeated the question. "Did you get him help?"

"We decided it was better if he parted ways with the church," someone said.

"You're saying you fired him."

"Yes."

Anger boiled up inside me. I'd had my issues with Neal, but there was no denying that he'd built Vancouver Community from the ground up. I believed he was a good man who wanted the best for the people there. And even if he wasn't, the people in this room weren't treating him the way Christians were supposed to be treating one another. I leaned forward, trying to address all four of them at once.

"Well, that's not what the gospel says, guys. That's not reconciliation. You're really telling me there's no path to forgiveness for this guy? *Nothing*?"

No one said anything. The looks on their faces were the same: all blank, mean, and superior—no different from all the neighborhood bullies I'd beat on as a teenager. Only now it was worse, because these people were bullying with nice shirts on, and they believed they were doing it because God wanted them to.

I leaned forward, feeling the brawler in me rear his angry head for the first time in years.

"Here's what's going to happen," I said. "We will agree to merge with your church. But before we do that, you're going to empty your savings and checking accounts, and you're going to write a check to Neal Curtiss for all the money you have. I don't care how much it is. I don't want to know, and I don't want my board to know. But you take *every dime* you have, and you write a check to Neal."

They looked back and forth at one another, then back at me. Their faces were blank.

"Second, we're going to assume all the debts and assets. I don't know how, but we'll figure it out. And third, you guys have to resign. Every one of you. And if you don't want to, then that's a clear no from me."

Even I was surprised by how direct I'd been. But I was angry. Something about the way these people, who were supposedly Neal's closest friends and colleagues, had turned on him in his hour of need made my blood boil. I hated the thought that they'd made him feel weak and cast out because he'd had the courage to come forward with his issues.

In the end, they did cut him a check for about $30,000, which kept him and his family afloat for a few months. I didn't tell him I'd been involved in making sure he got the money. Things were still a little frosty between us. But I did tell him that he was welcome to come back and work whenever he got his issues under control, and he always had a place at Living Hope.

A few days later I formally set down one of Living Hope's core policies. From now on we would seek out the most broken, damaged people in the world—the ones who, like me, had been made to feel like they were unworthy of a life in Christ because of their earthly struggles. I wanted to find each and every one of these people and let them know that at Living Hope, there was a place for them. I didn't care if they were drug addicts, pornography addicts, or alcoholics. I didn't care if they'd been to prison. All I cared about was whether they were willing to open their hearts to Christ.

I began putting the call out in my sermons, and people listened. As the months went on, more and more people began coming up to me after services with stories of the hardships they'd endured in life. I met people who took heroin every day but still found the strength to get up and come to church.

All the while, I was working with my team to expand Living Hope. I read stacks of books every night about business, trying to apply the principles to my congregation. We were growing so quickly that I could barely keep track of how many people were showing up each week. The shows we put on were bringing people from all over the Northwest. But despite our rich reserves of cash, banks refused to lend us money, citing a principle known as "catastrophic growth." We had no track record. Any day now, we could crash and burn.

One night I was flipping through a book on new business ventures when I came across the story of Howard Schultz, the founder of Starbucks. It was the early 2000s at the time, and these small coffee shops had begun popping up on every corner. I read about how Schultz, who'd come from nearby Seattle, had managed to take an idea that most people had scoffed at—a small storefront that sold a relatively cheap product and allowed customers to sit around for as long as they pleased without ordering anything—and turned it into one of the fastest-growing businesses in America.

That night I resolved to do the same thing with Living Hope. Soon we'd be everywhere. We'd expand even to the darkest corners of the world, where no churches had been able to succeed before. We'd lead even the most desperate, lost people in the world to Christ, and we'd put on a great show while doing it.

Soon I was working eighteen-hour days to make this vision a reality. If my team and I weren't writing sermons and staging my next wild spectacle for the weekend, we were poring over balance sheets and trying to find ways to spread the church all over the world. I was driven, as always, by my desire to help bring people to Christ. But I had also grown to love the business side of the operation. I wanted to put a Living Hope church within walking distance of everyone in the world.

We were well on our way. In 2007 *Outreach Magazine* ranked us the seventh-fastest-growing church in the nation. Our membership numbers were going up every day, rising above two thousand and officially earning us the designation of megachurch. At first I wasn't sure what to make of it. All I knew was that the crowds were bigger, and there was more money to reinvest into the ministry. The crowds were getting larger, and we were opening new campuses every few months.

On Easter Sunday in 2006, we launched four new campuses. In the year that followed, I drove back and forth between our main campus in Vancouver and those satellite campuses, preaching whenever I could. As the next Easter approached, I began thinking of ways to top it.

I prayed to God, asking for guidance. And He gave it to me, as clear as a bell.

Put a table on the stage.

The next week, I stood on the stage in front of my old kitchen table. I told people that we were about to do the offering, and that whatever money we got would determine what we did for our Easter service that year.

"Bring up here what God lays on your hearts," I said.

If it was only a few hundred dollars, we'd put up a few decorations and do a normal service. If it was more than that, maybe we'd make something amazing happen. When all the services were done, the money was counted. By the end of the weekend, we realized that we'd raised almost exactly $140,000, all of it piled high on my kitchen table. Whatever the Easter service was, I knew it had to be something amazing.

We had campuses all over town at the time, most of which ministered to a few hundred people every week. They were in storefronts and movie theaters, for the most part. I'd never seen everyone together at the same time, and I wanted to change that.

I walked around town one morning, looking for venues that could hold all three thousand of us. Eventually, I found myself looking over the river at a giant dome, and I knew I'd found the answer.

The Rose Garden.

Chapter 10

All my life, the Rose Garden Arena had towered over the city of Portland. The Portland Trail Blazers played there in the winter and spring, and the Winterhawks, our hockey team, took it over in the off-season. Over the years, I'd gone to basketball games there, marveling at the size of the place.

Now, forty days before Easter, I had a vision of a church service out on the hardwood. I walked straight into the office of the guy who booked the place and told him I was interested in hosting something there on Easter Sunday.

"Huh," he said, flipping through his calendar. "Looks like it's open for next year. What were you thinking about doing?"

"Not next year," I told him. "*This* Easter. Like the one forty-one days from now."

If he'd been drinking coffee, he would have spit it out.

"You're crazy," he said. "You understand that people usually book this place years in advance, right? You're talking about . . . I mean, how many people do you even have? You can't be serious."

I let him know we had a few thousand people. He reminded me that the Rose Garden was built for twenty thousand. He also told me that the deposit to hold the place would be almost $140,000, which was exactly how much we'd collected during Sunday's offering.

I thought of the passage in 2 Corinthians 5:13, in which Paul wrote, "If it seems we are crazy, it is to bring glory to God" (NLT).

If that's true, I thought, *I am about to bring a whole lot of glory to God.*

I brought him a check that day, and we had the arena booked as well as its three parking lots. In the lead-up to the Easter service, our talented staff and volunteers worked themselves to the bone. We barely slept. I planned to deliver a message on Matthew 7, one of the first chapters I ever connected with as a Christian.

More than 14,000 people attended the Easter service, and 683 people were baptized. Local news broadcasts did full stories on the sudden backup of traffic around Portland, noting that there were no major games or events at the Rose Garden that they knew of. A few minutes later, there were cameras everywhere. During the service, which I had titled "The Worst Day of Your Life," I quoted Matthew 7, which says that people who don't give their souls up to God—no matter what good deeds they perform on earth—will never be saved.

"On the day of judgment," I said, "these people will come to God and they'll say, 'I did all these good works,' or 'I was an elder at my church,' and God will say, 'Turn away from Me; I never knew you.'"

Allowing the message to sink in, I paused, staring at the thousands of faces out in the crowd.

"Now *that* would be the worst day of your life."

Lines formed in every aisle, and I prayed over hundreds of people as they began their lives with Christ.

I had never been happier.

By then, Neal Curtiss had come back to work with Living Hope full-time. He had conquered his demons, and I was happy to set him up with a job. Together with all the pastors, we managed to pull off one of the largest spontaneous baptisms in the history of the United States. To this day I look back on the mass baptism at the Rose Garden as one of the highlights of my life as a pastor. We would never see as many souls saved in one day again. We wouldn't even come close. And I couldn't have done any of it without the amazing team we had built.

It was also one of the last times I can remember being truly happy and satisfied with the ministry we had built at Living Hope.

Over the next few years I began to understand what the banks had meant by "catastrophic growth," which had always seemed like a strange phrase to me. Every time we opened a new campus, some of which were in far-flung places such as New Zealand and Hawaii, I would travel to speak at the opening; my body clock was completely out of whack. I was going to conferences all over the world, meeting my heroes. I spoke in India in front of tens of thousands of people, almost getting blown backward by the sound of them cheering all at once. I had dinner with people I used to listen to on the radio.

Around this time I learned that Reverend Billy Graham, one of the men who'd inspired me to start a church in the first place, was nearing the end of his life. I'd become close friends with his daughter Ruth Graham, a religion columnist for the *New York Times*, and I had attended one of Reverend Graham's crusades, although we'd never met officially. One afternoon I was at a conference in North Carolina at Reverend Graham's convention center. I had come along with dozens of other pastors from around the country. Ruth Graham was one of the organizers. Near the end of the event, Ruth let us know that Reverend Graham, who'd been scheduled to speak, wasn't going to make it. He'd been sick for some time. I was devastated, as I had been hoping to meet him at least once. But I didn't say anything.

Still, God was in control. My team and I were preparing to climb back into our rental car and head for the airport when Ruth approached me and asked if I would like to meet George Beverly Shea, a well-known pastor who was then 101 years old. He lived on the same mountain in North Carolina as Billy Graham, although their houses were separated by many acres. I said yes, and we went with Ruth to a sprawling complex high above Asheville, North Carolina. Reverend Shea played piano for me in his house and sang "Just as I Am," one of my favorites. He gave me a book, and we prepared to go back home.

"John," Ruth said. "Come here. Do you want to meet my daddy?"

I didn't realize at the time how rare this was. Although Billy Graham had ministered to every sitting president of his lifetime, only one of them had ever been to his home. I told Ruth that meeting Reverend Graham would be the honor of a lifetime, and off we went to his sprawling retreat, which sat just up the road. The moments that followed, which included some light conversation and a great deal of prayer at Reverend Graham's bedside, are among the most memorable of my life. It was as close as I've ever gotten to Jesus.

For years, Reverend Graham had been my hero. He ministered to people in a kind voice and led souls to Christ in a way that I had always wanted to emulate. He also had discipline, evidenced by his insistence that all televisions be removed from his hotel rooms when he traveled. Looking around his quiet room up in the Blue Ridge Mountains, I saw what a life of contemplation and following God could get you. Peace, quiet, and a loving family. I had no doubt that Reverend Graham was coming to the end of his life knowing that he'd done amazing things.

I, on the other hand, was beginning to get uncomfortable with how big my church was getting. The growth wasn't stopping, and I was having trouble dealing with it. New campuses popped up, all filled with parishioners who looked to me for guidance. One day, I was walking through the mall when I noticed an abandoned storefront that had been vacant for about seven years. By the end of that day, I was on the phone with the owner of the mall asking how much he'd charge me to rent the place. We settled on $4,000—which, I figured, was pretty good for eighty thousand square feet of space—and Living Hope moved again. Only now we were doing services right in the middle of a shopping mall, attracting not only our usual worshipers but also people who just happened to be passing by.

On Easter Sunday, we had Shawn Lewis, a Christian singer who was part of our worship team, do a few songs. A few minutes into the service, I was up onstage with him and his band doing an all-out rendition of AC/DC's "Highway to Hell" and rocking out with the band. It was as good a rendition as I'd ever heard, and it was going over well—sort of. From the stage, I could see the traditional Christians trying to run out the door while crowds of shoppers streamed in.

Then I saw a guy named Lance—who would later become one of my best friends—block the door and assure the fleeing Christians that there was a point to my madness. As the final chords of the song died out, I preached an off-the-cuff message about how many people are on the highway to hell when they don't have a relationship with Jesus Christ. I read a verse from the Gospel of Matthew that says, "Enter through the narrow gate. For wide is the gate and broad is the road that leads to destruction, and many enter through it. But small is the gate and narrow the road that leads to life, and only a few find it" (7:13–14). It was lighthearted at first, but also made a serious point—exactly the kind of thing I'd started a church to do.

As time went on, I began to feel like we were engaged in a never-ending game of Jenga. Just when I thought I couldn't take another block from the bottom and move it to the top, building my tower ever higher, I managed to pull it off. Every time that tower wobbled in the wind, I ignored it.

I was too high to see the bottom anyway.

Too high to see my son, David, who desperately needed his father.

By the time Living Hope became an official megachurch, David had been struggling for some time.

It began, as he'd later tell me, in middle school, when he and his friends used to smoke weed while they hung out at each other's houses. Other people could have a little and stop. But David quickly realized he couldn't. This was a story I'd heard often over the years, always from the addicts who came to Living Hope on the weekends. But I'd never heard it from my own son, who was struggling worse than any of them.

When he was in high school, Michelle and I sat David down, asking what we could do to help him. He said he felt lost and didn't know where to turn. We prayed with him, and he managed to get himself back on track for a while. I was extremely proud as I watched him get his grades up. One day he came to me and said he'd enlisted in the navy all on his own. He'd also scored in the top 7 percent of applicants on his entrance exams. Given the military background of our family, I was beaming as he shipped off to a naval base in San Diego. His mother and I prayed for him every night, happy that he seemed to be on the right path.

Things happened to David in the navy. In the interest of his privacy, I won't say more than that. But he came home even more broken than he'd been when he left, and he began taking drugs almost every day. He also started dealing, sometimes selling to the very addicts who'd come to Living Hope looking for reconciliation.

This ramped up in 2011, when Living Hope moved to our biggest spot yet—a large warehouse-style building that had once been a Kmart. While I was onstage facing crowds of thousands, David would be outside, doling out small baggies of meth, weed, and cocaine—as well as whatever else he could get his hands on—to addicts desperate for a fix. Unlike the mall, which was in a wealthy part of town, the Kmart sat in a more run-down area. Rather than continuing to put on the kind of massive services that we had at Prairie, we shifted our focus to serving the community. Amazingly, the crowd that had come to see all the elaborate sets at Prairie was more than willing to refocus their efforts and help other people.

Every week, we tried to come up with a way to use our resources to spread the Word of God and lift people up. This amazing group of people was willing to go out and be the hands and feet of Jesus. Incredibly, the church *grew* when we began serving the community. And so did our acts of service.

One of the most memorable events was a special needs prom, which we'd put on for anyone who hadn't been fortunate enough to attend their own high school proms. People donated dresses and shoes; beauticians volunteered their time and got everyone all dolled up for the evening. Michelle and I chaperoned for a while and danced. It was an amazing thing to see. We fed the homeless, took care of local schools, and organized charitable drives.

Meanwhile, David was suffering. And I was beginning to lose my grip on reality. The success of the church had gone to my head. By the time we'd been at the Kmart for a few years, I was ministering to thousands of people every weekend. My face was on DVDs that went out all over the world, and many people looked to me as a spiritual leader.

To make matters worse, my body was falling apart, specifically my knees. By 2014, the damage from all the fighting and power-lifting I'd done as a kid—not to mention all the theatrical sermons I'd been putting on since then—was causing so much pain that I had trouble even walking. I visited a doctor, who scheduled two knee replacement surgeries and prescribed me pain pills for the interim. But I didn't take them. I knew how devastating opiate addiction could be, having seen it firsthand with David and a few parishioners at Living Hope. I knew I had an addictive personality, and I didn't want to succumb. But the pain was excruciating. I could practically hear my bones grinding together every time I walked. One day, a friend asked me if I'd ever thought about having a drink to take the edge off.

I tried it.

It wasn't long before I was leaning heavily on alcohol again, succumbing to the same demons that had led my father to drive his car into a tree at the age of twenty-five. I drank beer at first, and then I graduated to vodka tonics. Over time, the vodka overtook the tonic, and I stopped using ice. It wasn't long before I was buying bottles of vodka and polishing them off before lunch. Since marrying Michelle, I'd had drinks only here and there. I also succumbed to temptations of the flesh, engaging in an extramarital affair with someone I didn't love.

To this day I consider this—not the drug dealing, the lying, or the many sins I would commit in prison, but the adultery—to be the worst mistake of my life.

I didn't have much time to dwell on what I was doing. Instead, I buried my feelings in alcohol, drinking to numb the pain and deal with the guilt. Even as I preached the gospel, I was lying to my wife and my children. I hated myself.

Around that time, I got a call from a police station in Vancouver. David had been arrested for dealing drugs. I drove straight to the station to pick him up. On the ride home, I wondered how things had gone so wrong. Somehow I had overcome the loss of my father and brutal abuse from my stepfather and come out the other side mostly unscathed. My son, on the other hand, had been dealt a pretty good hand by God, all things considered, and he'd ended up on the wrong side of the law.

Shortly after we moved into the Kmart, David entered prison. We were devastated. In the months that followed, I visited David in the small town of Forks, Washington, where he served most of his nine-month sentence. I even grew close with some other inmates who were in for similar issues, speaking with them about God, using my own upbringing to prove that it was possible to overcome horrible circumstances and survive. I redoubled my efforts to minister to broken addicts on weekends, speaking to my congregation as if I were speaking directly to David.

But the pressure was too much. Instead of dealing with it

directly, I ran away. I ran away internally by drinking and designing ever more elaborate missions for my church, burying myself in work because I couldn't face the demons of my personal life. And I ran away physically by visiting Living Hope's satellite campuses in far-flung corners of the world, believing that if I kept moving, I might be able to outrun the demons that were chasing me. I was willing to do anything other than confront my mistakes and my failings as a father.

In the ultimate show of arrogance, I wrote a whole book called *God Distorted*, which was built around the idea that our perception of our heavenly Father, God, is warped by the relationships we had with our earthly fathers. The book contains several sections about David and his troubles. Reading it today, I can sense how desperate I was to pretend everything was okay.

Near the beginning I wrote, "I know David has made wrong choices. Lots of them. I get it in my head, but I really have a hard time being okay with it in my heart. But then God lets me know that this is exactly why He wants me to write this book. He has me right where I need to be, learning exactly what I need to learn, in order to share what He wants me to share."

On the whole, the book is good. I'm told it's still taught in Bible colleges to this day. But the man who wrote it was deeply troubled, and he wasn't nearly as put together as the polished prose made him seem.

Almost every weekend, I was running to a different part of the world. Living Hope was opening campuses in different countries all the time. But the one I visited more than any other was in Cabo San Lucas, Mexico—a place which, for me at least, would soon become hell on earth.

Chapter 11

The first time I went to Cabo, I got a good feeling from the place. Michelle, who usually came with me on the early trips, always detected a dark undercurrent. But in the beginning, that undercurrent was deep under the surface.

And the surface was nice.

Almost everywhere we went, you could hear the ocean. Cabo was your typical breezy beach getaway full of gated communities and tourists who always seemed to be in the mood for a good time. Michelle and I walked the streets with big smiles on our faces, popping into restaurants, getting to know the locals. During a trip to one of our campuses in New Zealand, I got a call about a three-bedroom vacation home that was up for sale in a small community in Cabo. We bought it as an investment, although Michelle warned me against it. Back in 2006, that seemed like a good idea. Then, near the end of 2007, the economy entered a free fall, and the price of houses declined sharply. Michelle and I found ourselves stuck with the property.

Of course, it wasn't the worst problem to have. We spent most of the early years of Living Hope going down once or twice a year for vacations, staying at the house and getting to know our neighbors. We became almost like locals.

At the time, there was one Christian church in Cabo, called Cabo English Church. More than anything, it was a church for vacationers and short-term tourists like some of my neighbors. I don't think I ever saw the place full. Over the years, as I ventured farther into the more depressed parts of Cabo, I came to realize that no one was ministering to the poor people there. If you traveled more than a few miles away from the clean streets and solid houses near the shore, you came upon barrios that looked like something out of a disaster movie. People built their homes using sticks and blue tarps, sleeping underneath these rickety structures until the wind and rain blew them away.

We made a few attempts to engage in charitable work, but I learned quickly that the Mexican people do not look kindly on donations from outside their communities, especially if those donations come from white people. The people in town were proud. They were taxi drivers, restaurant workers, janitorial people, and waiters. All of the labor in town was done by Mexican people. And unlike in some of the run-down areas I'd seen in the United States, it was extremely uncommon to see people out on the street begging for money. People worked hard, and they resented anyone who came to town bearing handouts.

I soon realized that I wanted to be among these people. At first, we considered putting another Living Hope campus in Cabo where people could come to pray and spend time with other Christians. Soon, though, I came to realize that we needed to be down in the barrios, getting down in the mud and preaching in a language they understood. In the end, we rented an unfinished building between downtown and the barrios. We put up chairs and a modest altar. People began to show up.

Sometimes we'd drive down with tanks full of water to give out to people who didn't have their own potable water to drink. Teams of volunteers went down to Cabo from Living Hope all the time to put roofs on houses and make repairs to important things in the community. The residents were people with *real* needs. They worked six days a week, twelve hours a day, and still didn't have enough to make ends meet. We were happy to help. In time, Mexico became the place I visited the most.

Cabo was slowly becoming a second home.

And not just for me. As time went on, David began coming down to Cabo often, and we did a great deal of work with the church together. Sometimes, when we came upon people in the street who'd had a little too much to drink, we'd drive them back to their hotels and make sure they got to sleep okay. One Saturday night, we came across a guy who was stumbling around the streets, clearly drunk. David jumped out of our Suburban, picked the guy up, and loaded him into the back. Then we made sure he got back to his hotel. Just before we left the guy, he asked if he could pay us for what we'd done. David said, "No, just go to church tomorrow."

The next morning, we happened to see the guy walking into another church. I was about to go across the street and bring him over to ours, but David stopped me. "It doesn't matter *what* church they go to," he said, "as long as they're going somewhere."

Occasionally, when the work out in the barrios was done, some of my new friends and I would do work on my own house. These sessions were a little more relaxed, and they often included ice-cold beers and loud music. It was during these home improvement sessions that I became friends with some of the guys in town, whom I would come to find out were connected to the cartel. One of them was a large, affable guy named Israel.

Sometimes these sessions would turn into parties. Nothing crazy—just a few more beers for everyone, some music, and lots of talking about our lives. Guys I barely knew would show up, and I'd pull them right in to join the party.

One morning, after a party that had gone a little later into the night than usual, I walked out into my yard and found Jesus asleep in the driveway. (That's *Hey-soos*, pronounced the Spanish way.)

For a moment I thought the man lying face down in my driveway was dead. But I got closer, poked him with my finger, and the guy opened his eyes wide and apologized to me.

I got the impression that he wasn't a guy who usually drank a lot.

"Ah, sorry," he said. "Sorry, sorry."

He held out his hand for me to shake and told me his name was Jesus Martinez. I told him to come inside and have some breakfast. I'd been cooking up eggs and bacon anyway, and I was always happy to have company. Jesus stumbled in, rubbing his eyes, and sat at my kitchen table. He told me he was in business, and that he came down to Cabo once in a while to take in the sun. Most of the time, he lived at a house up in Ensenada with his wife.

Over breakfast, as we talked about our families, I got the feeling that we were cut from the same cloth. Our senses of humor were similar. We tended to approach life the same way. By the time he left that afternoon, we'd become good friends. On his way out, he warned me to watch my back around the cartel guys. He'd been around this town a lot, he said, and he knew what could happen when you got too close.

"They act like they're your friends," he said. "But they're not."

I told him I understood.

"No, John. I'm serious. I see guys all the time who come down here, and they get involved. They think it's all going to be great, because everyone is doing it. But it never works out. You go to prison for a long time. And eventually, you die. You *always* die."

"Jeez," I told him. "Pretty dark."

Standing there in the doorway, I got the feeling that I was in the first twenty minutes of a slasher movie—the part where the old man at the gas station warns the teens not to stay in the creepy mansion up the hill, which they do anyway.

And just like the dumb kids, I wasn't going to heed the warning.

As time went on, I made more connections in Cabo. Some of the guys told me straight up that they were affiliated with the cartel. Others didn't. But I still had a policy of turning no one away. Back home, I welcomed drug addicts and broken people of all kinds into Living Hope. Now that I was trying to make Cabo a second home, I stuck to the same mindset.

One Saturday afternoon we brought a few local people to the beach to baptize them. I took the first guy by the shoulders and explained what was going to happen, trying my best to get the message across via an interpreter I'd brought along. Together, the first guy and I walked out to the Sea of Cortez, and I went under the water with him. Somehow he slipped out of my hands and began drifting away. By the time I got up, he was fifty yards down the beach, kicking and waving his hands wildly. I ran down the shoreline with the thirty or forty people who'd come to watch the baptism, trying to tell him how to get back to shore.

He shouted something in Spanish, and I asked my interpreter what it meant.

"I can't swim," he said.

Finally, after a few panicked moments, the guy ended up in a shallow part of the water near the shore. We ran to him, and he held his hands toward the sky, yelling "Gloria Dios" ("Glory to God"). We embraced, and the twenty or thirty people who'd come along to be baptized all cracked up.

I turned around and asked who wanted to go next.

No one raised their hands.

After a while, though, baptisms became a regular feature of our services. It was wonderful performing them out on the beach in a natural body of water, just like the disciples had done in the Bible. I also enjoyed getting my hands dirty with our volunteers, working to fix whatever needed fixing in the homes of our parishioners. The needs of the people in Cabo, especially in the surrounding barrios, were overwhelming. Many people suffered from diabetes, and I visited their homes to bring medicine. We also tried to raise money to get people prosthetics.

One of the first things I noticed about Cabo was that outside of the main tourist areas, no one had shoes. Kids walked around in bare feet, stepping right in puddles, bloodying themselves on rocks and bits of broken glass. Sometime around 2015, when the church in Cabo was doing well and we had just added another building called the Ministry House to store all our construction gear, I heard about a little girl who'd died in the barrios. She'd been walking around in her bare feet, simply going about her business in the road, just being a kid. And out of nowhere, she'd stepped in a puddle that happened to have a live electrical wire in it. Within seconds she was dead, taken from her parents and her friends in a flash.

It was a moment that I couldn't get out of my mind.

Once I had seen her little face, I couldn't unsee it.

Shortly after ministering to that little girl's family, I went home to Vancouver and preached on a verse from Matthew about helping those in need. I talked about the little girl. Without realizing what I was doing, I said, "We can't do everything, but we have to do something. Why don't we . . ."

I paused, looking around for any idea.

"Why don't you take off your shoes and donate them? Or buy new shoes and donate those. These people are living without shoes all the time. Are we not able to walk without shoes from here to our cars? All of us have more than five or ten pairs of shoes, unless you're Michelle, who's got fifty pairs."

The room erupted in laughter, and people began bending down to take off their shoes. By the end of the service, I had a giant pile of shoes ready to donate. Over the next few days, that pile grew. Only then did I begin to try to figure out the logistics of what I was doing. At the border crossing, shoes were considered contraband. You couldn't simply drive over the border with a truck full of shoes (or used clothing or other items) and start handing them out.

But we decided to give it a shot.

In the end, my volunteers and I were stopped by customs agents with a trailer loaded with donated shoes. We had to turn back. Rather than giving up, I decided we were going to fulfill the mission slowly. I began having volunteers for Living Hope take vacations to Mexico, stuffing their suitcases with pairs of donated shoes every time they went. I was on a shoe crusade. I also went down to the border myself, "ant crawling" the shoes over in small batches.

As you might imagine, when you make the journey from pastor to drug runner, you don't do it quickly. It's not like flicking a light switch. It's more like a dimmer switch—the lights slowly go down, and down, and down, until finally it's black, and you can't see what's right in front of your face.

Waiting for the shoes to get across, I ended up in Tijuana for two weeks. The alcohol flowed freely. I stayed in locations that weren't good for me, including a run-down motel that was built on top of a cemetery. People back home told me to abandon the thousands of pairs of donated shoes and go home. But something—probably the fact that things were beginning to unravel in my personal life—made me want to stay and see the mission through. I felt compelled to do it.

So I made a few connections. I met a guy named Memo, who was the second-in-command for one of the major cartels. I met a guy named Victor Pelón (Spanish for Bald Victor) and a few of his associates. Everyone made sure the payments got where they were supposed to go, and the donated shoes slowly made their way down to Cabo. The Mexican police wouldn't stop trucks affiliated with Living Hope as long as they were getting the okay from the cartels.

The experience taught me a few things. First, that doing things for other people feels good no matter what country you do it in. Second, that *nothing* gets done in Mexico without the cartel knowing about it. And the cartel is a hands-on operation, as I soon found out.

One night, as I sat alone at my kitchen table down in Cabo, still running away from my family and career problems back in Vancouver, I heard a knock at the door.

And I found myself with a whole new set of problems.

The man was thin. He wore a nice suit under a scruffy beard. His eyes were dark and piercing, as if they'd seen things that would make you squirm.

"I want to talk to you," he said.

It wasn't a question.

Before I knew it, the guy had pushed himself inside my house, and we were sitting across from each other at my kitchen table. The guy—whose name, I would later learn, was Chucho—removed a 9-millimeter Glock pistol from his jacket and placed it on the table between us. His bodyguard, a giant Mexican man with face tattoos and arms the size of my legs, interpreted for him as he spoke.

"I want to find out what you're doing here," he said. "I want to know why you're here every week. Why do you go back and forth all the time?"

My eyes darted from Chucho to the bodyguard and back. I'd heard a little about the drug trade down here, and I knew what he was implying.

"No disrespect, man," I said. "But I don't want to die. Did I do something wrong?"

"Not yet. But if I find out you're selling drugs, I'm going to put a bullet in your head myself."

With that, Chucho got up and put his gun back in its holster. He left without a word, and his bodyguard followed.

Shaken, I poured myself a drink. I was no stranger to physical confrontation, but even I didn't think I'd stack up well against a bullet fired from that small cannon in Chucho's pocket.

At this point most guys probably would have booked the next flight home to Vancouver and put the Cabo house on the market. Looking back, I wish more than anything that I'd done that. But something about the way I was living at the time made me feel like I could stay. I was growing to like the guys I was hanging out with, and the small, rickety church (which I'd dubbed Laguna Cabo) reminded me of the early days of Living Hope, before the theatrical productions and the big crowds. All weekend, as I was preaching the gospel to thousands, I would dream of coming back to Mexico and cracking open another cold beer with the hombres.

The next week, I came back and asked around about a guy named Chucho.

"He's about this tall," I said, raising my palm about a foot over my own head. "He wears nice suits? Likes to put guns on people's tables and threaten to murder them?"

The guy I was talking to widened his eyes and shook his head. "Chucho," he said. "El Sicario. New Generation."

By this point I hadn't yet seen the film *Sicario*, which hit theaters in 2015. So I didn't know what the word meant. But the way my friend was shooting finger guns in my direction gave me some indication.

Chucho was a hit man. And he worked for the New Generation drug cartel.

At the time, the city of Cabo San Lucas was laid out according to which cartels ran it. Even tourists had to know the lay of the land. Around the beaches and gated communities, the Sinaloa Cartel was in charge. They sold weed and cocaine to gringo tourists on vacation, overcharging them for the product and putting on big smiles while they did it. The tourists, I learned, were where the money was. But once you stepped out of the main strip of Cabo, you were in New Generation's territory. They controlled everything from my house up to the border.

There wasn't much difference between the two, danger-wise.

But since the guy who'd come to me was from New Generation, I did a little research. I figured if Chucho was checking up on me, I'd read up on him a little too. After about five minutes I stopped. All I could find were stories about the New Generation guys murdering people in ways that would make Stephen King blush. They had cut out tongues and chopped off heads, raped women and stuffed men into barrels full of acid. Sometimes they hung corpses from bridges to warn other people not to cross them.

By then most people knew the story of the cartels. I didn't, but a few of my new buddies filled me in. Some of them were old enough to remember the 1980s, when the United States government trained rebels in Nicaragua, contributing to the rise of powerful groups that soon took over the country's drug trade. By the time I got to Cabo, the cartels were bigger than the armies of most countries, and they killed people every day. The Mexican police were effectively their military wing.

They owned everything from judges and cops to store clerks, businessmen, and prison guards.

Soon they'd own me.

"There are rules," said one of my friends. "The cartel never sends a sicario, an assassin, to do business in the place where he lives. If the cartel wants someone dead, they send a sicario from out of town to do the job. Always."

"Where's Chucho from?" I asked.

"La Paz."

"Which is . . ."

"Out of town."

About a week later I heard another knock.

Chucho.

I opened the door and found him standing with a new bodyguard.

I was about to ask what happened to the last guy—probably knowing the answer—when he pushed past me and stepped into the house, a big smile on his face. The new bodyguard followed.

"Good news," he said, pronouncing the phrase in English. "I . . ." He switched back to Spanish, which I couldn't understand. I looked at the bodyguard.

"He wants to go upstairs with you," he said.

Chucho began climbing the stairs and motioned for me to follow. The bodyguard stayed where he was, almost like he was watching the door.

At the top of the stairs, Chucho turned into my bedroom. I followed. He closed the door and stood facing me for a moment. Then he put a hand on his chest and began grasping for words in English, a big smile on his face.

"My heart," he said. "You, me. I *love* you. And I know you are not dealing. And now we are going to celebrate."

He reached into his jacket.

I braced for a gun.

Maybe he's just calming me down, I thought, *getting me up to the bedroom where there's a tub to cut up my body.*

Maybe he's going to use a knife.

Maybe the bodyguard already shot me and I'm in hell right now, living in this suspended moment of tension for eternity.

But instead of the Glock, he pulled out a small baggie of white powder.

Cocaine.

I'd never done coke, but I'd seen it enough to recognize it. Standing in my bedroom, watching Chucho carve up the powder into thick lines on the thick wooden foot of my bed with a shiny razor blade (*What else had that been used for?*), I thought of David. Coke, I knew, had been his drug of choice for a while, before he had switched to meth.

"I've never done that before," I told Chucho.

He smiled, showing me a row of bright white teeth.

"For me, you will."

Chucho leaned down and snorted half the coke through a rolled-up hundred-dollar bill, sucking up every last bit like a Hoover vacuum cleaner. He leaned back and let out a satisfied grunt, just like the drug lords in the movies. I picked up the bill, which had come unrolled when Chucho threw it across the room to me, not even sure how to go about getting the powder into my nose.

"Would you mind if I just . . . ?"

I scooped up a little coke with my finger and rubbed it on my gums. It was something I'd seen guys do in movies when they wanted to test a product's quality. Right away, I felt a numbness and a head rush, mixed with something that felt like taking six beers through an IV. Chucho laughed at me, like I was a kid trying a spicy pepper for the first time.

"Fine, fine. Yes."

We talked for a while, Chucho going a mile a minute in coked-up broken English that reverted to Spanish at the ends of his phrases. We went downstairs to the kitchen. The bodyguard gave up trying to translate. Later, I'd learn that the two of them had rented the house next to mine, sitting at the window and watching me as I came and went. Probably watching me walk around the house and get ready for bed every night too. When the guys left, I ran straight to the bathroom and tried to wash my mouth out. But the head rush from the coke wouldn't fade.

I stayed up most of that night, staring at the ceiling, wondering what the hell I'd gotten myself into.

Chapter 12

At home, rumors swirled.

It was November 2015, and the church was bigger than ever. We were putting on four services every weekend, baptizing hundreds of people, serving the community however we could. I had begun running the place like the writer's room at *Saturday Night Live*. Every Wednesday we'd meet to flesh out ideas for the service. From there it was nonstop, stay-up-all-night work to make sure we put on the best service we possibly could. I wanted every service to run like it was the last one we'd ever do.

But I noticed that people were no longer meeting my eyeline during meetings. The volunteers were less enthusiastic. When I threw out an idea, it would be met with muted nods and mumbles of agreement. Someone was poisoning the well, trying to turn my own team against me.

And I had a feeling I knew who it was.

I found Neal Curtiss in his office, the one I'd arranged for him to move into when he came back to Living Hope full-time, which had a desk and a couch and a bookshelf and a nice wheely chair.

He was sitting in that chair when I stormed in and confronted him.

Over the past few days I had heard shocking allegations from my daughters. They said Neal had pulled them aside and told them I was screwing around on their mother in Mexico. He claimed he'd seen a picture of me kissing some woman at a bar in Cabo, which I knew couldn't have existed, because I'd never done such a thing.

When I asked him to produce the photograph, he stammered. I thought about him praying over me when I was a twenty-five-year-old kid bleeding from my nose, remembering the confident tone of his voice as he asked God to look after me. I thought about the moment he'd asked me whether I thought I was going to heaven and led me to Christ. Physically, Neal was the same guy I'd always known. But inside, something had shifted in him. His demons had taken over. And fortunately for him, those demons didn't make him do outwardly horrible things the way mine did. There would be no fighting, drinking, or snorting coke with Mexican hit men for Neal.

What he had, though, was jealousy. So much of it that it practically leaked out of his eyeballs. Suddenly I remembered the way he'd gone cold during our first phone call about Living Hope Church. I remembered all the moments he'd watched me preaching from the back of the room with a strange look in his eye, as if he didn't understand why people didn't react to *him* the way they reacted to me. All along, he'd coveted my position as the head of Living Hope, and he'd waited for his moment to take it from me.

Somehow I managed not to let my anger come out in a negative way. I didn't even bother to tell him what I probably should have: that being at the top of Living Hope was not anything he (or anyone) should aspire to. The top was lonely. It was confusing. And it made you do things that had the potential to ruin your life.

Instead, I turned and left his office, speed-walking past dozens of people who all eyed me with suspicion.

I walked into my own office and locked the door, then pulled out a water bottle full of vodka and unscrewed the plastic cap.

I drank until I fell asleep.

Then I woke up, and I drank some more.

For a while the cold blackness that settled over my mind was comforting. It felt like oblivion, which was what I wanted. The voice of God—the one that had led me to make every good decision I'd ever made—was quiet.

Somehow I preached to seven thousand people that weekend without slurring a single word. But the story I chose to preach was revealing. I told the story of Elijah, a prophet of God who'd been told in the book of 1 Kings to flee for his life. Elijah was running from Queen Jezebel, who had sworn to kill him for defeating the prophets of Baal. He was exhausted, scared, and ready to give up. But God sent an angel to provide him with food and water, sustaining him as he traveled forty days and forty nights to Mount Horeb.

In that lonely cave Elijah cried out to God, overwhelmed by despair and convinced that he was the only one left who was faithful. But God's message was clear: "Go back the way you came. You're not alone, Elijah. There are still seven thousand in Israel who have not bowed to Baal." God had provided for Elijah every step of the way, even in his rebellion, to remind him that he was never truly alone and that his mission was not yet complete.

In a strange way, I felt like I was running to the end of myself the same way Elijah was running to the end of himself. And God was sending more distractions to keep me running.

I hadn't found the end of myself yet. I wouldn't find it for quite some time.

A few days later Michelle confronted me about the affair.

I knew she'd found out because Neal had told her. But I couldn't be mad about it. For all his scheming and lying behind the scenes, he was right on the fact that mattered. And the fact that mattered was that I had betrayed the one person who'd always believed in me, stuck by me, and loved me no matter what I did.

Breaking down in tears, I told Michelle the truth. It was a short fling with a church employee that had been over for months. I had been drinking so much in part to cover my guilt and to stop myself from breaking down every time I looked at her.

Michelle was devastated, as I had expected her to be. So were my daughters. All along, I maintained that the other lies Neal had been feeding people about me weren't true. But my family had trouble believing me, which was understandable. I prayed with them for hours, and we called a meeting of the church elders. I decided I would go to rehab for a few weeks to kick the drinking habit. I would also spend some time alone praying, trying to work my way toward forgiveness. I knew the elders all knew the gospel, which provide a pathway for even the worst sinners to be redeemed. I knew that Neal, who was sitting against the wall during the meeting, knew all about that pathway to forgiveness. Without it, he'd still have been living in a small house and selling mortgages to get by.

About two weeks later, I packed up my things and checked into a rehab facility in Ventura, California, which specialized in the cases of famous scumbags like me. I cleaned floors, shared my story in group therapy, and managed to stop the shaking from alcohol cravings after just a few days. Michelle, still understandably upset with me, kept in touch via text and email. From rehab I reached out to an organization known as the Association of Related Churches (ARC), hoping they would step in and help Living Hope reorganize in the wake of the scandal. Over the years I'd grown close to a man named Greg Surratt, who preached at one of the most influential churches in South Carolina. I figured he might be able to help. But there wasn't much ARC could do. During the first meetings with the current leadership of Living Hope, they were fed lies about me. A small group, led by Neal, accused me of stealing money from the church (charges of which I was later acquitted by a full IRS forensic audit as well as two other audits by two other federal agencies, but no one knew that at the time). One day Michelle let me know that Neal Curtiss had approached her and said he was going to take the church leadership and start a church two miles down the road if she didn't step off the board. All she could think about were the people at the church who'd be abandoned if Neal followed through on his threats. Eventually, she was fired.

As far as ARC—and the world—were concerned, I was toxic. So was my family. Even as I attended my group meetings and tried to put myself on the road to recovery, we were being pushed out of the congregation we'd started in our living room twenty years earlier. Worse, we were being pushed out by people we believed we could trust. Our friends. Our neighbors. People who'd been over at our house and sat at our table and asked us for help during the darkest times of their own lives. I thought about leaving rehab and going home to fight for my family. But Michelle shared an email she'd received from the ARC leadership, who were by then our only hope of staying on as the leaders of our church.

"If John leaves treatment," it read, "we will not support anything going forward with Living Hope."

So either I stayed where I was and gritted my teeth while my church was stolen from me, or the church would dissolve.

I decided to stay where I was, praying for a miracle, knowing deep down that I didn't deserve one.

The emails came early in the morning on December 15, 2015.

We were being fired. All six of us. My daughter Katie; her husband, Jordan; and their two babies were forced to vacate the church-owned mobile home they'd been living in. Another church leader needed the space for her family. My son-in-law Cody, who'd just been in a life-threatening car accident, was going to lose his medical insurance. There would be no severance pay. No path to coming back for any of us.

That same day, Michelle was ushered to her office by a staff member and forced to pack up her things. She took some of mine too. A few hours later a team of church volunteers went into my office and tossed everything in it into a dumpster behind the church. Tapes of every sermon I'd given, copies of all my books, and handwritten notes for my messages all went into the trash. Ironically, so did the only existing copy of the manuscript for my latest book, which I had tentatively titled *Too Soon to Quit*. The book, which was set to be published by Random House the following year, told the stories of people who'd almost given up, making the case that it was always too soon to quit on your dreams.

When news of my firing reached Random House, they quit on me, canceling the contract and asking me to return the money they'd paid me for the book. And they weren't the only ones. When I emerged from the rehab facility clean and sober a few days after my termination, I had almost no messages from the people who'd been with me for almost twenty years. My phone was as quiet as it had been during those first weeks with Focus One. I felt like I had no friends in the world.

There were exceptions, of course. While I was still in rehab, I got a message from a young guy named Kevin, with whom I had worked on hundreds of projects over the years. He was like a son to me. On the night Neal had the volunteers throw out my things, I learned, Kevin had gone dumpster diving to save them. He'd managed to recover dozens of boxes and hard drives as well as the full collection of DVDs that contained my earliest messages.

I thought about going over to Kevin's house to collect all the material. For years, my first instinct had been to get to work. But I no longer had a job. My flock had moved on, and there was no one to preach to. I decided to focus on my family, which I had broken into pieces during my never-ending search for personal gratification. Everything else, I assumed, would fall into place if I could simply make amends with the people who'd always stood by me. At the very least, I figured the darkest days of my life—the heavy drinking, the brushes with danger, and the constant waiting to be found out—were over.

I had no idea what was coming.

Chapter 13

I left the rehab center in Ventura with a single bag and my Bible. My head was clearer than it had been in months, which only served to sharpen the self-loathing I felt. Everything that had happened over the past few months—the drinking, the affair, and the brushes with the cartel—had become crystal clear during those long nights in my cot. I'd passed the time writing sermons no one would ever hear and studying the Bible, hoping to find a way out of my suffering. I asked God what to do next.

But I couldn't get an answer.

Michelle met me at the airport. Seeing her for the first time felt like coming home, even in the middle of this hot, unfamiliar city.

We didn't even think of going back to Vancouver, where our friends and family were. The pain would have been too great. Even the thought of driving through town, past the community center where she'd celebrated her sixteenth birthday and the stadium where I'd preached to thousands of people just a few years earlier, put a sick feeling in the pit of my stomach. I wasn't ready to face everyone yet. I couldn't go home to Vancouver, where everyone knew my name and my face.

So we checked into a hotel near the airport. Michelle spent most of the night with her face in a pillow, sobbing uncontrollably. In all the years we'd been married, I'd never heard her cry the way she cried that night. It was as if all the anger and shame she'd been holding on to since she began to suspect me of having an affair were finally coming out. Although she'd been the picture of composure in the weeks since, mostly to look out for me and my health, her breaking point had finally arrived.

I held her most of the night, feeling awkward and guilty. I didn't know what to say to comfort her. Words, which usually came so easily to me, failed me.

What could I say?

I had hurt the person I cared most about in the world, and then I'd gone to rehab to take care of myself. Michelle, on the other hand, hadn't gotten a break. She'd stayed at the church dealing with all the drama and the treachery. She'd been forced to carry her things out of her office all alone. There was nothing I could say that was going to take that away. All I could do now was keep the promise I'd made to her to quit drinking for good and to work every day to earn her trust back, even though she'd told me I didn't need to.

The next morning, we woke up early and sat in the room. We tried not to talk about what had happened.

We both agreed that we couldn't go back to Vancouver. Things were still too raw there.

So we bought two tickets to Cabo San Lucas, Mexico.

The sea air was nice for a while.

For the first time in years, Michelle and I had nothing to do and nowhere to be. We woke up whenever we wanted to and took long walks along the beach. We prayed every morning. Whenever I would run into someone from the cartel, I'd introduce them to Michelle as a "business guy" or an old friend from my ministry down here. She didn't seem to suspect anything. But behind the scenes, I was beginning to feel the pull.

The cartel knew I was down bad. Rumors about my split with

the church had spread through town, and I noticed a change in the way the guys were looking at me. I was desperate now. If they were sharks, I was a slow fish with a bloody, broken fin.

It was only a matter of time before they got me.

Once, when Michelle was at work—she'd gotten a job in San Jose, not far from our house—Chucho and his bodyguard came by the house. He didn't bother putting his gun on the table this time. But I knew it was there, tucked into the inside pocket of his jacket where it always was.

"Papa John," he said, using the nickname that had, by now, become known all over town.

"Chucho."

"Sorry about what happened to you."

"Thanks."

He leaned back and smiled.

"You still drive back and forth to the US, yes?"

"I mean, yeah."

"We have an offer for you."

For the next five minutes Chucho laid it out for me. Given that I was an American—and a pastor at that—I was trustworthy in the eyes of the border patrol. I could, if I so chose, buy a car in my name and drive it over the border every day, pretending I was just commuting between California and Tijuana. Thousands of people did it every day. So many, in fact, that there was a special lane at the border for them called SENTRI. This lane had decreased security. Anyone could slip in and drive over the border with anything in their car.

I asked Chucho what he had in mind.

"Silencers," he said.

I must have looked confused, because he took out his own gun and started to show me, holding it sideways and pretending to screw something onto the front. "You put them over the gun, and it makes them quiet. You know?"

I'd seen enough action movies to know what he was talking about. I also knew that you didn't use them for hunting or casual shooting at the range. You used them when you wanted to kill someone and not have the neighbors hear it.

Behind Chucho, his bodyguard laughed.

"You want me to smuggle silencers for you?"

"Yes."

"What do you . . . I mean, *how*?"

"We'll take care of that," he said. "You just have to get in the car, drive, and drop them off where I tell you. And you'll make good money. Which you need. Yes?"

I leaned back in my chair, thinking it over. I looked over at the clock on the stove, trying to calculate how long Michelle had been gone and when she might be back. It was true that we needed money. I was now making zero dollars a year, and Michelle was still studying to be able to sell time-shares. We had our savings, which wasn't much, and the equity in our house in Vancouver, plus this time-share. The cars were gone. Our retirement savings were minimal. During the boom years at Living Hope, I didn't think the money would ever stop. I had assumed, like the opposite of the man in the parable of the rich man, that I would always have time to save. Now I was desperate.

But not desperate enough to traffic weapons for Chucho.

Not *yet*.

"No way, dude," I told him.

Over the past few months he and I had gotten more comfortable around each other. We'd had drinks out at bars. I'd listened to him tell me about some of his problems, and I'd told him about mine in turn. We were almost friends.

Still, the look that came over his face at my refusal was troubling. I looked at the hand that held his gun, looking for any sign of movement. But nothing came.

"You're sure?"

I nodded.

"Fine," he said. "But if you change your mind . . ."

He got up and his bodyguard followed. For the first time, I got a look at the guy: the same one who'd been there during Chucho's second visit with me. There was something about the way he looked around the house that creeped me out. Although I'd been around some serious people before—drug dealers, pimps, cold-blooded killers—I had never gotten the sense that real evil was present.

Until now.

Chucho and his bodyguard stepped out of the house, leaving a chill in the air. Michelle stepped back in not too long after and asked me what was wrong.

"Nothing," I said.

No matter what happened, I was going to protect her from these guys. She was never going to know the kind of company I kept when I came down to Cabo alone. Putting my own life in danger was fine with me. I didn't think much of my own life anyway. But putting the lives of the people I loved in danger was too much. I wouldn't do it.

I still believed there was a way for me to exist in that town without having to cross paths with the cartel in any real way. I'd gotten to know some of the guys pretty well, and I had come to know them as people created in the image of God, not just by the jobs they did (most of which happened to involve murder and drug dealing). I assumed I could stay Papa John, the kindly minister from the United States, without any real repercussions.

I was wrong.

After a few weeks of aimless wandering, Michelle and I started to have some fun in Cabo. We knew that there were resorts along the water that did special tours for visiting Americans. All you had to do was show up and pretend you were interested in buying a time-share, and you'd get a free breakfast and some cash. Michelle and I decided to give it a shot.

Sure, we told everyone we spoke with that we didn't have money to buy anything. But it was harmless, and it was a good time. After all that we'd been through, I figured we needed to blow off some steam.

Walking through those resorts on the water, seeing all the happy couples, enjoying our free eggs and engaging other people in light conversation, we recaptured a little of the magic that we'd lost. It was nice being able to sit down together without having to worry about the next giant event we were going to stage on Sunday. One morning, as we sat in a beautiful beachside restaurant at some resort, it hit me that I hadn't had a drink in months. And I didn't want one. Being here with my beautiful wife was enough for me, even if I didn't have a clue what I was going to do with the rest of my life. Sitting there in the sunshine and talking with her made me feel like we were teenagers again, sitting in that back booth at Denny's while a waitress walked by with a half-full pot of coffee trying to make us leave. I felt like after everything, we were finally falling in love again.

I was happy.

For a moment, it felt like we could get back on our feet. I had applied to a few jobs, and things looked good. We'd made some money selling all the crap we'd acquired over the years: my guns, some stereo equipment, furniture.

We were going to make it.

Eventually, the little vacation period came to an end.

So did the time-share adventure.

Someone recognized us, ran a background check, and realized that we already owned a house down the road. That morning, we ran away like a couple of kids, giggling about the stupid prank we'd managed to get away with. To this day, we're not permitted to set foot in several luxury resorts around Cabo. But those weeks of screwing around had cleansed my palate a little. I finally felt like I was ready to get back into preaching and start rebuilding my life. When I saw guys from the cartel out in public, I ignored them. I no longer spent my nights out drinking and hanging around. I'd been granted a fresh start, and I wanted to use it.

Sitting in the kitchen one day, I came across an app called Periscope that allowed you to stream live video to people all over the world. I'd experimented with similar things before, never with much success. But this seemed like a way to begin flexing my muscles again. Every morning, I'd pick out a Bible verse and write up a few notes on it. Then I'd set up my phone, begin preaching, and watch the number of viewers climb. I was talking to a few hundred people after the first few weeks, and the messages were flowing in. If I closed my eyes, I started to feel like I was back onstage at Living Hope, delivering God's message while fireworks went off around me.

Although it didn't seem like it sometimes, I was only ever interested in giving God glory. I didn't care about getting famous myself, even if I did start to like it after a while. Sitting with Michelle and talking to a few hundred strangers over the Internet was enough for me. All that mattered was the impact I might have on the lives of the people watching and listening. If I could save one person, that was enough.

As it turned out, saving one person would be my next mission.

For legal reasons, I can't say much about this period of my life.

All I can tell you is that in the middle of 2016, a wealthy person reached out to me and asked if I'd come to his ranch and meet with his son. This kid, whom we'll call James, was in trouble. Like many children of rich, successful fathers, James had never quite found his way in the world. He didn't have many friends or a girlfriend. Over the past few years, he'd been in and out of eight treatment centers without showing a single sign of improvement.

Sitting down in the family's massive living room, I could tell that James wasn't an addict. He was just a deeply confused kid who didn't know where he fit in the world. I talked to him about treatment centers, given that I'd just been in one myself, and we got along well. I've always prided myself on an ability to talk to anyone. By the end of the meeting, the father had offered me $7,000 a month to minister to James and help him come out of his shell.

There was no real job description. I just needed to make the kid better. At the time, it wasn't lost on me that I hadn't even been able to do this for my own son. Although David was doing better than before, he still hadn't been able to kick heroin. As I sat in the beautiful, well-appointed house of this wealthy man's family, David was bouncing between Vancouver and Mexico, staying with Jesus Martinez and making connections with street thugs in Ensenada. I didn't like that. But I trusted Jesus—whom David called his "Mexican dad"—to keep my son out of trouble while I scraped my life back together in the United States. That, I realize looking back, was more than anyone could handle.

Over the next few months I tried to help James overcome his issues. We traveled all over the state he lived in, talking about what he thought was wrong with him and how he might fix it. I quoted the Bible to him and prayed with him. After so many years of ministering to thousands of people, I was now ministering to only one. And it went fine for a while. James seemed to be making progress. He didn't touch a drink or drugs the whole time I was with him.

Then, one morning, his mother pulled me aside.

"I know he's not an addict," she said. "What he needs is to have some fun. Find him some friends. Find him someone to . . . *you know.* Anything."

For a moment I wondered if they'd hired me because they believed I knew how to have a good time. I thought about telling them that I'd been sober for a few months now and having a good time was the furthest thing from my mind. But I didn't want to get fired. Seven grand a month was a lot of money, and I had genuinely come to care for James.

We started by going to a couple of bars. I sat in the corner with a seltzer while James sipped beer and tried to make small talk with strangers. Afterward, we'd critique his performance and talk about what he could do better next time. It really was working for a while. Away from his parents, he was finding himself in a way that he probably couldn't while they were around. As time went on, I had to critique him less and less. He was getting good at talking to people.

One night James asked me why I wasn't drinking. I told him I had some serious problems with alcohol, so I'd stopped. Given that the kid had been to eight treatment centers, I figured he would understand. But he didn't. Or he *pretended* not to.

"You can't have one?" he said.

I shook my head.

"*One?* Are you kidding me?"

Something in my addict's brain lit up. I really *could* have just one. To this day, I don't think I'm an alcoholic (which is kind of the problem). I ordered a beer and sipped it.

When it was gone, I ordered another one.

Then another one.

It took exactly five minutes for me to fall off the wagon and become a crazy drunk again. I was partying all the time. James and I would go to clubs, and he'd rent out the VIP section with his dad's credit card. By then, he'd kicked the whole shy thing like a rented mule. He was talking to everyone in the bar, chatting up girls without fear and buying drinks for everyone. I had, in some sense at least, done my job.

At least that's what I told myself as I downed eight beers a night in the corner, then switched to shots of vodka when the music got loud.

Late one night when the bar was about to close, James got up on a stool and invited everyone back to his dad's place a few miles away. To this day, I don't know how everyone got there.

Over the next few hours, this kid threw a party that put my little fiestas in Mexico to shame. Girls danced on tables. Guys did coke in the bathroom. By the morning, when his parents got back from a trip, the place looked like we'd used the house to film a real-life remake of *Animal House*.

Before I knew it, I was hungover in the driveway, and James's dad was screaming at me. Apparently, he and the wife hadn't coordinated about exactly what I was supposed to be doing. Dad still believed I was here to help his son kick drugs and alcohol. Mom, on the other hand, wanted me to take him out partying so he could make some friends.

Unfortunately, Dad was the one in charge of cutting me checks, and his wife hadn't let him know about the conversation we'd had a few weeks earlier. Instead, she'd thrown me under the bus and backed over me ten or eleven times.

"You need to go," said Dad, pointing at the open road.

What do you mean? I wanted to say. *You flew me here, dude! I barely know where "here" is!*

Instead, I let my anger take over.

"I don't know, man," I said, stepping toward him. "You might need to make me leave. Because I am not happy right now."

He didn't move.

"Fine," he said, all full of rich-guy confidence. "Stay here. I'll call the cops."

I changed my mind on kicking the guy's ass in about half a

second. He looked serious about calling the cops. And I knew that the story—as you can tell, because you just read it—would not make me look great.

I learned later that I was right: James was not an addict. He was, in fact, dealing with serious mental challenges, but he wasn't an addict. I haven't spoken to him since the night of the party.

Today I view my time with him as nothing more than another shameful episode in a life that's jam-packed with shameful episodes. I've recounted it here only to help you understand just how far I'd fallen after getting fired from my church. I wasn't kidding when I compared myself to Elijah, who ran for hundreds of miles in the desert, fortified by bread and water sent straight from God. Every day, I ran further from the truth of what I'd done. And every time I stopped to catch my breath, somebody was there with more beer and more vodka to fuel my flight from accountability.

As I left the wealthy man's ranch, I had already hit more rock bottoms than most people can even dream about. And I knew I wasn't done. As John Milton put it in his epic poem *Paradise Lost*, "In the lowest deep a lower deep/Still threatening to devour me opens wide/to which the Hell I suffer seems a Heav'n." Even then, walking down the road alone trying to hail a cab in the fall of 2016, I could feel something rumbling beneath my feet.

A lower deep, threatening to devour me.

It was only a matter of time before it happened.

Chapter 14

After the episode with James, I tried to go back to Cabo and recapture a little of the magic with Michelle. But it was gone. I was drinking again, swearing that I could control it this time. She wasn't having it.

Before I knew it, I was back in Vancouver.

David would come around sometimes. But he spent most of his time down in Mexico, making inroads with the cartels. I'd check in on him when I could, but there was no talking him out of spending time down there. He was an adult, after all, who was making his own decisions. I trusted Jesus Martinez and a few other friends down south to keep an eye on him for me. For a while, David was down in Mexico with all my friends, and I was back in Vancouver with his friends, mostly my former parishioners from Living Hope.

One of the friends who came around was a former parishioner named Greg. He'd been around Living Hope in its heyday, although he didn't attend church anymore. I'd known him since he was in his late teens. I'd even baptized him. One night, hanging around the garage the way he'd done with David when they were kids, he mentioned that he needed a car. I asked him to follow me out to the driveway.

There, parked in the place where our three cars used to be, was a 1996 Toyota Camry in forest green. My grandfather had bought it brand-new. When he died, he left it to my mother. A few weeks after I was fired from the church, my mother dropped the car in my driveway, along with an envelope full of crisp hundred-dollar bills from her savings. I'd planned on returning the money to her. But in the weeks since she'd been by, I'd spent almost all of it. We had no income. No savings. I had taken the parable of the rich man a little *too* literally, reinvesting all my money into the church rather than storing it up for later in life.

I never thought the church would abandon me.

Now I had nothing, and I saw a way to make a few bucks. I pulled the keys to the Camry out of my pocket and dangled them in front of Greg.

"You could rent this from me," I said. "It was my pop's, so I know it's well taken care of. Not many miles on it, either, considering how old it is."

I thought about all the days I'd spent riding around with Pop as a kid, watching him take the turns carefully, always going one mile an hour below the speed limit. I missed him. I wanted to recapture the feeling I'd gotten when I saw him walking up the aisle toward me to receive Christ, tears in his eyes at how proud he was of me. Now I was back at rock bottom, feeling the pull of an even deeper one in my gut. It felt like I had barely progressed from the hoodlum the cops had dropped off on his doorstep. And now I was renting out his car, the one thing (other than who I am as a person) that I had left of him.

Greg said he'd take the deal.

"How about a hundred bucks a month?"

"Three hundred," I countered.

"Two."

I thought about it. Just a few months ago I could have leased this kid a brand-new Range Rover. I probably *would* have, if he'd asked me to. Now I was haggling over a hundred bucks, and I needed every dollar of it.

"Deal."

He drove off in Pop's car, and I stood watching the taillights disappear, folding and unfolding the ten twenty-dollar bills he'd given me.

Then I went inside for a drink.

From my kitchen counter, where I sat with a full glass of vodka and ice, I could see empty spaces all around the house from the stuff we'd sold. The house was emptier than it had been since the day we bought it. I knew we had only a few months left before we had to sell it. I'm sure that if I wanted to, I could have found a way to make an honest living in town. I had skills as a carpet cleaner and a businessman. I could have worked as a bartender or a cashier or a real estate agent. I could have written another book or looked for work as a pastor.

But I couldn't face all the familiar faces around town. Every time I went to the bank or stopped in a restaurant, I'd see someone who knew everything about me. Back in the days when I was the hotshot pastor of the fastest-growing megachurch in town, this was fun. I'd talk for hours with people I'd grown up around, missing appointments and basking in the glory that came with having escaped my rough upbringing. Now I'd proven that I was no better than my father or my uncles. Worse, even. Showing my face in Vancouver was like walking around with a big Failure sign hanging from my neck.

So instead of finding an honest job, I stayed inside. I drank. I brooded. Every day took me further from God. Every day made me more desperate.

That summer Michelle began losing her patience with me. We weren't speaking as much, and we slept in separate bedrooms. David let me know things were going well for him down in Mexico. I heard rumblings of his involvement with a few high-level cartel guys. I hoped Jesus Martinez was looking after him.

Then I looked down at the cash I had left. I figured I could leave it on the counter for Michelle and the family, or park it in our dwindling bank account so we could use it to pay bills. Or, I thought, I could use it to get back to Mexico—the one place in the world where I was still a pastor, where no one cared about my spectacular fall from grace.

The next morning, I was gone.

Part 3

PAPA JOHN

Chapter 15

I was sitting at my favorite taco stand, a place called Pice's, when a car pulled up outside. It was around four o'clock in the morning, and the taco stand was crawling with people. I had come with my friend Black Victor, a lieutenant in the cartel, after a long night of drinking and partying in the barrios.

"Papa John!" someone yelled. "I know you're in there. Your son owes me money."

The voice was slurred, but the English was pretty good. I got up, my mouth still full of chicken and tortilla, to see what was going on. Black Victor followed a few steps behind me. Outside, idling in the middle of a busy two-lane road, was Fish, a local thug who was high up in the cartel. Through the tinted windows of his car, I could see he had four or five guys with him.

"What's going on, man?" I yelled from the sidewalk, feeling the eyes of everyone in the taco stand on me.

By this point, most people in town knew who I was. Most importantly, they knew I was friends with the man who ran all of downtown for the Sinaloa Cartel—whose name, oddly enough, also happened to be Victor. (We called him Victor Señor.) That was supposed to keep me safe. Low-level thugs like Fish weren't supposed to pull up to taco stands and call me out in front of crowds.

But here he was, hanging his arm out the window of his car,

watching with a demented smile as his boys walked toward me with menace in their eyes.

I walked straight toward the car, pushing past them to get close to Fish.

"How much does he owe?" I asked.

Fish opened the door and got out.

It wasn't until he raised himself up to his full height that I realized he was at least five inches taller than I was. Probably fifty pounds heavier too. I tried not to blink, knowing I'd have to fight him if it came to that.

I watched him trying to calculate a number in his head.

Finally he said, "Seven hundred bucks."

It sounded like a scam to me. The kind of thing that guys in the cartel would try if they thought they could get away with it. Which, unfortunately, they usually could. At this point, I wasn't working for Victor Señor. I was just a guy who hung around and entertained him and his buddies. For some reason, the cartel guys liked me. I made them laugh, and I listened to them tell me about their problems. That offered me protection.

But only so much.

David was a different story. Although he'd gotten so close with Victor Señor that he was living in his house up the road, he hadn't made himself many friends among the low-level cartel guys like Fish. That was largely because David was a talented drug dealer and a charismatic guy. Everywhere he went, people loved him. That was especially true of white tourists, who were always happy to buy drugs from David that they never would have bought from some of the cartel-connected Mexicans in town. There was a gated community up the road called Pedregal, where celebrities and well-connected Americans vacationed. Unlike the locals, David could slip in with no problem, charming the guards at the front gates with a smile and a little small talk, then sell drugs to the residents.

I don't know whether it was jealousy or real hatred that made the cartel guys go after David so hard. Maybe it was just because they knew messing with him was a good way to get money out of me. Which, sadly, it was. Every time I heard that David had run into trouble—whether that trouble was real or cooked up by the cartel to cause problems for my family—I would do whatever it took to get him out of it. I guess it didn't take long for everyone in town to figure out the game.

Hence Fish, standing over me outside the taco stand and shaking me down for seven hundred bucks.

"Fine," I told him. "Let me figure it out."

As soon as Fish and his guys drove away, I got in the car with Black Victor and headed up the road to the small house where David was staying with Victor Señor. Along the way, we passed crumbling buildings and a run-down gas station, swerving to avoid drunken tourists along the road. Unlike some of the top-level cartel guys, Victor Señor didn't live in a mansion on the water. He lived here in the barrio, hiding in plain sight. At least a dozen members of his family shared the ragged compound with him. David had been living there a few months, too, burrowing himself even deeper into the world of the Sinaloa Cartel.

No wonder these guys are jealous of him, I thought as we pulled up to the house. *They're slinging weed and cocaine for a few bucks per transaction, and David—some gringo no one had heard of a few months ago—is living with their boss's boss's boss's boss.*

Inside, we found David and Victor Señor in the living room. A few other people walked around, carrying beers and cracking jokes.

I explained the situation, and David said it sounded familiar.

He'd owed Fish a couple of bucks months earlier, and the price had gone up since then.

Victor Señor asked me what I could pay.

I reached into my wallet and counted out all the cash I had. It amounted to something like $400.

"Good," said Victor Señor. "We'll say four hundred."

He picked up the phone and called Fish. They exchanged words in Spanish. I grabbed a couple of beers for me and Black Victor, and we sat down on the couch.

In the next room, where Victor Señor had wandered as he spoke, I heard him conclude the conversation with Fish.

"Mi casa," he said, coming back into the room. "Mañana." *My house. Tomorrow.*

Black Victor and I left.

David stayed at the house with Victor Señor.

Very early the next morning, I slipped out of bed and headed back to Victor Señor's house, slightly dazed and ready for our meeting with Fish. As the sun glared down on the barrios, Victor Señor and I drove in his hot-rodded Mustang to an empty street on Squid Row. David didn't join us. After several minutes, a few guys gathered around, almost enough for a crowd. I had flashbacks to my uncle's backyard, where I'd stood in similar circles and pummeled people for entertainment. Given Fish's size, I hoped something similar wasn't about to happen. But I was ready for anything.

Fish pulled up a few minutes after the appointed time in a run-down Nissan Sentra. Victor Señor got out of his car, and Fish got out of his. They walked toward each other as I watched from the passenger seat of the Mustang. In my hands I held the four hundred bucks I'd promised. Victor Señor motioned for me to come over, and I watched Fish's guys from last night get out of their car as I did.

Victor Señor held his hand up and told me to stop walking.

The crowd parted.

Suddenly I felt like I was in a Clint Eastwood movie, standing about twenty feet from Fish with a crowd watching in silence all around us. I yelled something at him about how he'd brought his guys. We were supposed to meet alone. He narrowed his eyes, the scowl on his face deepening.

Victor Señor held up his hand and said, "Go."

Fish and I walked toward one another slowly.

I transferred the money to my left hand and made a fist with my right, knowing my only shot at winning this fight—if it even *was* a fight—would be to hit first and hit hard.

But when we got close enough to hear each other speak, Fish stopped.

"Papa John," he said, almost whispering.

I was taken aback.

"Fish," I said. "How are you?"

Like I'd just run into an old friend at the grocery store.

"Good," he said, surprising me by speaking English.

"Good. We settled on four hundred?"

"Yes."

I handed it over.

"I only have one request," I said.

He asked what it was.

"My only request is that you don't ever sell drugs to David again. Don't give drugs to David to sell, and don't ever let David go into your debt ever again."

He looked back at his guys, then back at me.

I could feel the crowd hold its collective breath, likely knowing that this was their last chance to see a good fight this morning.

"Fine," he said, holding out his hand for me to shake.

And then something came over me.

I knocked his hand sideways, took three steps forward, and wrapped him in a bear hug.

"See that?" I said. "You're a good guy, man! You're a good guy."

Much to my surprise, he hugged me back.

The crowd cheered and clapped.

And then, I assume, they went to their houses—or to the bars around town—and spread the story. I can only imagine what it sounded like. Victor Señor and I went back to his house to let David know that everything was taken care of, and we laughed about the whole thing. But I had a feeling I hadn't seen the last of Fish.

Or guys like him.

That night I went to a run-down bar on a side street in Cabo. In the past year, I'd become a regular. Sometimes, on the increasingly frequent occasions that Michelle came down for a visit, I would wait until she went to sleep and then head out for a drink (or ten).

As usual, I drank a few beers, then a couple of vodka sodas. Anything to bring on the dull, all-encompassing buzz I needed to bury my problems. Then I'd sit at the bar talking to whoever came in, listening to their issues and doling out fatherly advice as it came to me. I'm sure I looked ridiculous. By then, I was beginning to put on some weight from all the tacos and booze, and my eyes were usually bloodshot.

Slowly the regular patrons left, and a new crowd entered the bar. Same as every night. The music got louder, and the faces around the bar changed. Someone eyed me and said something to me in Spanish. The tone was halfway playful but also laced with a little menace.

I walked over to the far side of the bar and punched him in the stomach.

We squared up, and a crowd surrounded us.

The Secret Cabo Fight Club, in which I had become a kind of folk hero, had begun.

I bobbed and weaved to avoid the guy's punch, stumbling a little from the vodka. He landed a right cross to my chin, and I felt a dull ache, knowing it would hurt like hell in the morning. Out in the crowd, someone screamed. They didn't like when I got hit. Even though I came from out of town, I was kind of like the home team. Cheers erupted as I charged the guy and pummeled him. I didn't have anywhere near the speed I'd had in my uncle's backyard. But I still had power, and I still had size. Most importantly, I still had that anger deep inside me, more intense now than ever because of how royally I'd screwed up my life.

But it wasn't anger that drove me to fight. It was the comfort of stepping into the ring, having an opponent, and shutting out the real world. In the brief moments that I had a guy charging at me with his fists raised, my crumbling marriage didn't matter. Neither did the church that was falling apart in my absence or the son who was still running around Mexico, making friends with the wrong people. Sometimes you have to feel pain just to feel *something*.

I'm told that there's a hierarchy to the way the brain deals with pain. Small injuries can seem devastating until a bigger one comes along. If you're dealing with chronic leg pain, whacking yourself in the hand with a hammer can make it go away for a minute. There are only so many circuits in the nervous system that tell your brain, *Ow, this hurts*. This, in a sense, is what I was doing with the fights at the bar: distracting myself from the dull, creeping horror that waited for me outside on the streets of Cabo.

That night, I won. This wasn't unusual. Again, there was no prize for beating the other guy. Just the respect of the other patrons in the bar, many of whom were connected to the cartel in some way. Most nights, my opponent and I would end up drinking with our arms around one another, recapping the brawl like it was a Las Vegas title fight. I'd tell him he was quick; he'd tell me I had a good right hook. We'd make plans to get hammered and fight each other again soon. I have no doubt that most of the guys I was fighting back then were dealing with some of the same problems that I was—a faltering marriage, childhood trauma, or trouble with the cartel. For some reason, we all dealt with it by fighting.

And people took notice.

By this point, word had spread about how I'd faced off with Fish out in the barrios. I had a little street cred. As I left the bar with a handful of ice pressed to my temple, sometimes leaving a trail of blood behind me, I could hear whispers and murmurs about who I was and what I was doing in town. My legend, such as it was, had begun to spread far and wide. In time, everyone would come to learn about the gringo pastor who had, largely by accident, made friends with all the top members of the Sinaloa Cartel.

Who ran a church in the barrio with cold beer and handed out shoes to kids in need.

Who, depending on the day, would punch you in the face or wrap you in a big bear hug and tell you that you were a great guy.

I'm sure most of the people who heard these early murmurings about me could tell that I was headed for trouble—and probably prison.

But I sure didn't.

All I knew was that I loved the Mexican people and that messing around in the barrios was a lot more fun than going back to Vancouver, where my wife was trying to sell our house and salvage our reputations among friends and neighbors. So I kept hanging out, kept fighting, and kept inching closer to the most dangerous guys in town, waiting for whatever was coming next.

During the spring of 2016, I still held services every week. I still put out buckets of cold beer for the guys, spending the last of my meager savings on showing my congregation a good time. Sometimes I'd have parties at the house, and cartel guys would come by. During one of these parties, a crew I recognized from around town pulled me aside. I braced for a punch in the face or a gun to the head, but they seemed shaken.

"You know Chucho?" one of them asked, speaking in broken English.

I looked over at the kitchen table, where Chucho and his bodyguard had threatened me all those years ago, when I was still a pastor with a thriving congregation. A shiver ran up my spine at the memory.

"Yeah," I said. "Is he here?"

"He's dead."

I gasped.

I don't know why. People died all the time around Cabo. It wasn't an outwardly dangerous place like Tijuana or Nayarit, where you could hear gunfire as you drifted off to sleep every night. But behind all the sandy beaches and giant resort buildings, there was a seedy underbelly. Bodies piled up quietly in the night, and the local police—who, like everyone, were on the cartel payroll—swept them away by the morning.

"What happened?" I asked.

"Shot," said the guy. "Eleven times. In the face. By his own bodyguard."

I thought back to the guy who'd come into my house behind Chucho. The mean, blank look in his eyes. If even a bigshot like Chucho could get gunned down in the street, I knew no one was safe.

Especially not me.

"You preach, yes?" said the guy, slipping back into Spanish.

"Well, yeah."

"We are doing a funeral. Tomorrow. You lead it."

I thought about Jesus Martinez's warning.

They always die.

Always.

But Jesus wasn't here. These three dudes were. And I liked the feeling of being needed again. Especially for preaching.

"Sure," I said, pretending I had a choice. "Let's do it."

The next morning, a car pulled up to my house. Two guys in suits got out and put a black bag over my head. As they guided me into the back of the car by my shoulders, telling me to watch my head and step carefully, I wondered whether I had seriously misjudged the situation.

Maybe *I* was the one who was about to get eleven bullets to the face.

Maybe I'd beaten up the wrong guy at the bar, and someone had decided I needed to go.

I knew that killing me would be nothing to these guys, like swatting a fly that had been buzzing around their faces for too long.

But the sound of cocked hammer never came.

We drove in silence for about twenty minutes, the fabric of the bag making my nose itch like crazy, before I spoke.

"You know," I said, trying to keep a friendly tone. "It might not be my place to say it. But you guys *really* can't be doing this kind of stuff."

A voice from the front of the car asked what I was talking about.

"Killing people in the streets. Gunning people down like this. It's . . . I mean, for one thing, you can't kill people. That's in the Bible. And for another thing, it's bad for business. I know lots of gringos who come down here to Cabo because they think it's safe. They like the beautiful beaches and the nice resorts. If they start seeing guys getting shot eleven times in the face a mile from their resort, they're going to stop coming. And if they stop coming, you know, who are you gonna sell drugs to?"

It was the first time in a long time that I'd slipped into my relaxed, free-flowing preacher voice.

It felt good.

"Yeah, yeah," said one of the guys to my right. "We know. Thanks, Papa John."

As far as business consulting advice for the cartel went, that was all I had.

Driving over bumpy country roads with a bag over your head tends to unsettle the stomach, and by the time we got off the exit for La Paz, Chucho's hometown, I was ready to puke. I stepped out of the car onto hard sand, and someone removed the bag. The bright sunshine made my eyes ache. It was the same feeling you get when you walk out of a movie theater back into a sunlit afternoon. Only now, I felt like I was walking *into* a movie rather than away from one.

There was a hole in the ground. About a dozen men in black suits stood around it with their hands clasped in front of them. There were women and children, some crying, some staring straight ahead. I walked up and greeted them in the best Spanish I could muster, which probably wasn't great. Then I took my place at the head-end of the coffin, just like I'd done hundreds of times before.

Across the hole from me, I spotted a kid who couldn't have been more than four years old. I thought of my dad, whose funeral I didn't even remember. Was this kid going to remember laying his dad to rest? Would he think all his life about the strange white guy who showed up with a bag over his head and said prayers over the coffin?

But my thoughts were interrupted as I looked out at the landscape: brown sand and thickets for as far as you could see, tiny white crosses dotting the landscape like flecks of dust. Each one of those crosses, I knew, represented someone who'd been killed and buried just like Chucho—guys whose deaths had come at them in the middle of sunny afternoons, or at night while they were sleeping. They'd gotten knives in their ribs or bullets in the backs of their heads. Or worse. And now they were resting under unmarked graves, far from their friends and their families.

Standing out in the desert praying, I knew I could be next.

David could be next.

The thought made me shiver as I shook the hand of Chucho's widow. She mumbled something to me in Spanish, and I blessed her and her children.

My escorts and I got back in the car, and the bag went back over my head.

It was nearly dusk by the time we got back to Cabo. I stepped out of the car with the guys who'd brought me, and we went to a bar for drinks. At the bar, one of them pulled me aside and started talking business with me. He referenced the little speech I'd given them in the car, and he said he agreed.

"You're right, Papa John," he said. "We can't be doing stuff like this. We're not going to have anyone left to sell to."

That word—*we*—caught my attention.

I kept sipping tequila and telling stories in broken Spanish. The guys loved it. When I think back on that night—and all the other early nights in Mexico—one phrase sticks out to me. As time went on, I'd hear it all the time.

Papa John, you're one of us, man.

You're one of us.

Chapter 16

"I have an opportunity," said Andreas. "If you want it."

We were sitting at my house drinking beer. In the past year, I'd grown close with Andreas, who spent most of his time driving tourists from the airport to the resorts along the beach in a taxi.

He, like almost everyone else I knew in town, was affiliated with the cartel.

By this time, I was completely broke. Michelle was back in Vancouver, living on food stamps and help from friends and relatives. My odd jobs brought in enough money to eat but not much else. I asked Andreas what the opportunity was, treading lightly.

"Just driving," he said. "You drive across the border with some product, and we'll pay you. Three grand."

I took a sip of beer, considering it.

"You're a pastor," he said. "So you get across easier than we do. And you're white, which helps. They'd take care of everything, man. Get you a nice car, tell you when to cross, when the friendly guards are going to be on lookout. It's just driving, but you do it with a little extra weight in the car. It's nothing."

"What's the product?"

He winced a little. "Marijuana."

"No."

Over the past few months, I'd been approached several times about trafficking stuff over the border. Chucho, may he rest in peace, had asked me about silencers, and I'd refused. Others had raised the possibility of trafficking heroin, and I'd told them no every time. The drug had torn my family apart. I wasn't going to help anyone bring more of it into the United States.

We hung at the house for a few more hours, drinking and talking.

I was planning to keep doing day jobs until I could get a big ministry together in Cabo. I figured I could build something similar to what I'd had with Living Hope, only without all the theatrics and expensive set pieces. I saw myself operating on a shoestring budget, ministering to the people in the smaller villages around Cabo. Many of them still didn't have shoes. Even water was scarce. Every day, I saw something that made me want to give away everything I had—which, again, wasn't much—to heal the pain that these people were clearly feeling.

"We could help with that," said Andreas, who'd listened to my plans more than once. "You could get a ministry going around here. With our help."

The implication was clear.

Work for us, and we'll help you out.

You can be one of us.

I told Andreas I'd think it over, and he leaned back and smiled.

"That's good, Papa John," he said. "That's good."

Wherever I turned, the cartel was there.

One night, walking back from the bar, I got jumped by a gang of six or seven guys on the road. I was still deciding which one to punch first when they got me on the ground and took my wallet. When I got up, I realized my phone was gone too.

I didn't even need to tell the cartel what had happened. Later that morning some guys showed up at my house with my phone and wallet. All the money was back inside, plus a little extra. One of the guys who'd come by told me how they'd tracked down the thieves and beaten them bloody. They had pictures and everything. I tried to be appropriately thankful, but in the back of my head, alarm bells were going off.

Those bells got louder with every day I remained in Mexico. One afternoon, I walked into the house to find David sitting with a girl named Johanna he'd been hanging out with. Right away, I noticed that she had a black eye. I asked what happened to her, and she let me know that a low-level street thug named Lulo had punched her in the face during a fight. Apparently, he didn't like that she was spending so much time around David. Once again, I felt the familiar sense of righteous anger that had always come over me when I saw people being bullied. I went downtown looking for Lulo, wanting to talk some sense into him.

I didn't find him. But I did find a guy named Posado, who owned a radiator shop. He was a big guy, and we had become acquaintances over the years. I mentioned what had happened to Johanna and said I didn't understand how someone could do that to a woman. I gave up looking for Lulo, and I didn't think much of it.

That night, I heard a knock on the door. I opened it to find Posado and one other guy. Between them was a man with a bag over his head, just like the one the cartel had put over my head when I performed Chucho's funeral. The only difference was that Lulo's bag had been secured with duct tape. Posado and the other guy dragged Lulo into my house and threw him onto a rickety chair from my kitchen. David and Johanna ran into the other room. I watched as Posado pulled out rusty metal instruments of torture and a gun.

"What do you want to do?" he asked me, holding a scalpel.

His voice was exactly the same as it would have been if we'd been talking about a repair on my car.

I held my hands up and said, "Whoa. Let's all slow down."

Posado looked confused.

"I don't . . . I mean, let's take the bag off his head, for one thing."

The bag came off, and I saw that Lulo's mouth had been taped shut.

I told Lulo it was nice to meet him. Much to my surprise, he nodded at me calmly. Johanna came around the corner into the living room, and she sat on the couch. I asked if he'd hit her, and he said yes.

For the next twenty minutes, I slipped back into pastor mode. We spoke about why violence against women was wrong. Lulo promised that he'd try to keep his anger in check. Every few seconds, I'd glance over at Posado, who was still holding his metal knife, looking a little sad that he wasn't going to get to chop someone's finger off today. In the end, they untied Lulo at my urging and allowed him to leave. I felt that I'd handled the situation about as well as I could have, given the circumstances.

The cartel guys stuck around for a while, and we talked about why I didn't think violence was always the solution to problems. They didn't seem to agree. When they left, I reflected a little on how strange it was that *I* was now the one urging people to settle down and not act out of impulse. I also realized that I was coming to like most of the guys I was spending time with, even if they were hardened criminals.

Then it hit me: These people had recovered my stuff after a mugging. They had tracked down a guy I had a problem with and dragged him to my house with a bag over his head.

I owed favors, and I had a feeling the time to collect was coming.

My front door was open.

I stepped inside, ready to confront a thief or a vagrant. When I called out, a familiar voice answered.

"In here, Dad."

David.

I found him sitting on the living room couch with bruises on his face. Beside him, a skinny guy sat with a gun on his lap.

"Your son screwed up," he said.

I looked around. The television was off the wall, lying screen-side-down on the carpet. Five guys stood nearby, looking around the house for other things to steal.

"Okay," I said.

After the incident with Fish at the taco stand, I'd learned a few things about dealing with scumbags like this guy. The first was that they respected strength. Flinch once, and they'd walk all over you. Luckily, my number one rule about fighting still applied: I couldn't walk away. Because of that, I'd developed a kind of reputation. These cartel guys might have thought I was a frail old man who could easily be taken advantage of, but they also thought I was crazy. They'd see me lay beatings on guys twice my size, and for all they knew, I was apt to go nuts and start cracking skulls at any moment.

Maybe they were right. I was getting hit in the head a lot back then, and I walked around all day with a coiled rage inside me. Even I didn't know what I was capable of.

"You're lucky," said the guy, leaning forward as he ran his finger over the handle of the gun. "Because me and my family like you, and we like David, you're going to be okay. We just need you to do a job for us."

David looked at the floor.

I wanted to grab the guy's gun and beat his teeth in with it.

"Same deal that Andreas gave you," said the guy. "Only we'll double the price. Six thousand. All you have to do is drive a car up to Vancouver, your hometown. Easy."

Clearly, these guys had heard that I was beginning to soften up. The floodgates were open, and the sharks were swimming through.

I asked what would be in the car.

"Heroin," he said.

I refused.

David's eyes went wide. He hadn't grown up around bullies like this guy, so he didn't understand that deep down, they were all weak. Corner them, and they always caved. That didn't mean the guy wasn't going to come back soon with a few dozen friends and beat my ass. But it meant that for now, there was nothing he could do. He wasn't going to shoot me. If he did that, they'd have to find a new gullible old man to mess with. And those didn't come around nearly as often as you might think.

The man left. David stayed and put ice on his face.

I picked up what I could around the house as he leaned back with his eyes closed. He apologized. I told him it was okay, that we'd figure it out. I wished I could put him in the car and take him home, but he'd been part of a drug bust in Vancouver a few months earlier, and given his prior record, he believed there was a warrant out for his arrest. Going home meant going back to prison. In Cabo, he had friends. He had Jesus Martinez and Victor Señor. As long as he stayed on the right side of the cartels, he'd be fine.

If it meant keeping him safe, I would work for the cartel. I'd smuggle weed. I would do almost anything if it meant keeping my son from harm.

But David wouldn't have it.

"You can't handle this, Dad," he told me. "Get out of here. Go home."

We hung around the house for a few days after that, always looking out the window for guys with guns. David took off once his face had healed. No matter what I tried, I couldn't stop him from getting back out on the streets. I could overpower him physically, even with my weak knees and slow reaction time, but I couldn't just hold his head down on the carpet forever. The pull of his addiction was too strong to keep him in the house for very long. Eventually, he'd end up back out on the street, dealing drugs and smoking meth. His teeth were tiny nubs of what they'd once been; his limbs were as thin as they'd been before he went to prison. Watching him walk out of the house, I'd always face the possibility that it might be the last time I saw him. Every time my phone rang, I wondered if this was the call that would let me know he'd been found face down in a ditch somewhere.

Little did I know that David was just as worried about me—and with good reason. For months, he'd been listening to the high-level guys at the cartel talk about me. He knew that they saw me as a dumb gringo who'd eventually do their bidding if they made me the right offer. While I was running around town handing out money to every thug who told me David was in danger, my son was working behind the scenes to keep me away from the bad guys. He knew I was in a vulnerable state and that it was only a matter of time before I said yes to the wrong people.

Which, a few weeks after the break-in, is exactly what I did.

I was sitting in my house with Andreas, drinking beers and hanging out, living the same *Groundhog Day* life that I'd been living for months. I was making plans to open a bar in Cabo or to start a fishing charter. In the back of my mind, I knew none of these plans would ever come to fruition. But talking them through felt good.

Andreas made me the same offer he'd made months ago. I would drive some weed over the border, and I'd make about three grand for my trouble. All I'd have to do was allow the cartel to purchase me a car (which I would pay off later), put the car in my name, and get approved for SENTRI. The rest, he assured me, would be easy. I eased myself back in my chair, took a sip of beer, and took stock of my situation.

I had nothing. Back in Vancouver, Michelle was preparing to sell the house, which would soon be foreclosed on. My cash was running out, and every day I was getting offers from low-level cartel guys to run drugs (or guns, or whatever) over the border. I sincerely believed that my son was in danger almost all the time and that my getting close with the cartel might keep him safe. I had no idea how wrong I was about that.

"Sure," I said. "Why not? Just let me know what to do."

"Good," said Andreas. "When you're ready, we'll go see a guy named Pablo."

I asked who that was.

"He runs things in Tijuana. No one ever meets him. He's like a ghost. But if you want to work running drugs, you'll have to clear it with him first."

I thought that sounded fine.

"I just have to get home first, back to Vancouver," I said. "We have some stuff to deal with. But I'll hook up with you early next year, and we'll get going."

I flew home a few days later. Walking through the airport past tinsel and shiny holiday decorations, I tried to forget about Mexico and everything that had transpired there. I wanted to be with my family and to regain some sense of all that I'd lost.

It was a few weeks before Christmas, and I had just signed a deal with the devil.

Chapter 17

Over the years, I'd put on some amazing Christmas celebrations. Early on at Living Hope, I had led the congregation in almost every Christmas carol we knew. Once we moved to the bigger venue, we'd put on a living nativity featuring Hannah, my youngest daughter, and her boyfriend, Cody, who would eventually become my son-in-law. Donations always poured in by the bucketful after those services, and we'd used the money to support various charitable organizations around town.

In December 2016, things were different. Michelle and I had just declared bankruptcy. Some rooms in the house were almost completely empty because of how much of my stuff I had sold to support us. Even my grandfather's car was gone. Greg hadn't answered any of my texts about bringing it back, even though he still sent me money for it every week via Venmo. To my great shame, we relied on charity from my mother, who was living on social security, to buy groceries and get by.

David did end up coming home. I was happy to see him, but I was distraught about not having enough money to buy gifts for my family. My daughters told me it was okay. They remembered all the years that I had gone crazy with gifts, trying to make sure they'd still love me.

Now that he was back in Vancouver, David settled back into his old life. Most nights, he'd have an old friend over, and they'd do drugs in the garage. I was too burnt out myself to do anything about it. If anything, I was happy he was staying at home and out of trouble rather than hitting the streets and linking up with some of the dangerous people who'd led to his imprisonment a few years earlier.

Sometimes I'd walk into the garage, which I'd converted into a library with about seven thousand books, and say hello. One night, I walked into the garage later than usual and saw David passed out on a couch. His eyes had rolled into the back of his head. A hypodermic needle, a spoon, and a lighter lay on the coffee table beside him. The friend, whose name I won't disclose here, sat with him, indulging in less potent drugs so she could stay up and make sure David didn't overdose.

It's hard to describe the sight of your son—a living person you've known since he was a nine-pound infant with gray-blue eyes and tiny, strong hands—destroying his body with drugs. More than anything, I wanted to reach David and save him. In that moment, I would have given up all the success I'd ever had with the church if it meant I could save my own son. Guilt paralyzed me as I knelt down and ran a hand through his hair, seeing the tips of his thin, rotten teeth as his mouth fell open.

All these years, I had been focused on anonymous addicts out in the crowd, trying to save people I'd never met while building the church. Meanwhile, my son was struggling at home, and I had ignored him. Even as we took family vacations and went to Seattle Seahawks games together, I wasn't giving him the support he needed to conquer his demons. There were times when things seemed to be going well. David had performed amazingly in Christian youth theater along with his sisters. He'd managed to get a scholarship to college, which he gave up only so he could join the navy. But something had gone wrong. Addiction had taken hold. Standing over David in the garage that night, I felt no better than my own father. In some ways, I felt worse. If I had died when

David was four, he might never have spent his life around all the broken people he ended up falling in with; he wouldn't have been able to deal drugs in the back of my megachurch. He might have grown tough from the loss the way I had.

I turned to the friend and asked what David had taken.

"Heroin," she said.

"Give me some," I told her. "I want to know what it's like. I want to know what David does."

At the time, this made perfect sense to me. I saw my failure to connect with David as a failure to understand him. I assumed the best way to fix that was to put myself under the spell of addiction that he'd been under since he was a teenager. I believed that my own issues with alcohol paled in comparison to the ones David had been dealing with all his life.

And I was right.

The friend asked whether I was sure, already heating up a little more heroin in a spoon. I said yes. She drew the heroin from the spoon into a needle and began searching my arm for a vein. I said I didn't want it in my arm and asked if there was another way to do it. She broke off the needle and held it near my head.

"Tilt your head back," she said.

I sat down and did what she said. She pried my eye open with two fingers and let a few droplets fall from a syringe, right into the skin of my eye.

The rush was immediate. I wasn't even done blinking away the tears when I felt a bomb go off in my guts. Even the rush from Chucho's cocaine didn't compare. For a fleeting moment, which felt to me like it was an hour, I felt all my problems disappear. My brain flooded with chemicals, and I began to feel that everything was going to be fine. I understood how someone—particularly a person who was lost and scared like David—could get addicted to this feeling. Right away, I craved more. But the craving was overshadowed by a deep, stomach-churning nausea.

I ran out to the side of the house and puked. Then I puked some more. By the time I stumbled back into the garage, the floor seeming to shift beneath my bare feet, David was awake and screaming at his friend.

"What the hell?" he said. "You got my *father* high?"

It was good to see a little energy from my son. Since getting out of prison, he hadn't exactly been lively. Most mornings, he woke up and drifted between rooms, looking for his next fix with a deadness in his eyes.

I sat in a chair against the wall, running my eyes over the spines of the books on the far side of the room. To my surprise, the rush that I'd always assumed would come from taking heroin for the first time wasn't there. *Nothing* was there. Just oblivion, and a creeping darkness at the corners of my eyes.

I gave in and drifted off to sleep.

The next morning, David confronted me.

"This is a bad drug, Dad," he said. "You can't be doing it."

"I wanted it, son," I said. "I asked her to give it to me. I want to understand your life. I want to understand your world. And if this is what I have to do, this is what I'm going to do."

Again, the logic of it made sense to me at the time. What can I say? I'd just had heroin dripped in my eye. That's not the kind of thing that improves your critical thinking skills.

David shook his head and paced the garage. But I could see I was reaching him. Finally, after all these years, I was preaching right to *him*. I wanted to help, and he could sense that I was willing to do anything—even the most dangerous drug on the planet—to get down in the mud with him and bring him back up. For the next few days, we hung around the house, not doing much of anything. Michelle was usually asleep by the time either of us got up and moving. At night, one of David's friends would come by, and they'd shoot up in the garage. I'd stick with my beers, which I considered perfectly fine for a clean and sober person.

At least it's not a fifth of vodka, I thought.

But it wasn't much longer until I *did* drink a fifth of vodka. Then another, and another after that. Looking around at the house we were selling and all the empty spaces where our things had once been—looking through old drafts of my books and notes for messages that I had always intended to deliver—made me miserable. Every day, I came across more evidence of my failure. I felt terrible for betraying Michelle by drinking again. The only thing in the world that I had to hold on to, oddly enough, was the relationship with my son, who seemed to finally believe I could help him.

Every day leading up to Christmas, David and I would sit and talk for hours, far more than we'd ever spoken when we crossed paths in Mexico. I'm sure that it had something to do with the fact that I was beginning to live a similar lifestyle to him—hanging around, not caring very much what the consequences would be in the morning. But I clung to that relationship. We both did. Neither of us seemed able to defeat the demons that lurked in our blood—the ones that always drove us to have another drink or another line of cocaine, or to stay up long after everyone else had gone to sleep.

The same demons, I knew, that had killed my father and so many people he knew.

I decided that I was going to help David. Although I wasn't willing to do heroin again, I was going to stick with him and let him know that he didn't have to be shy about his addictions around me. I was going to stay right down in the darkness with him. With any luck, we'd make it out together.

In the days leading up to Christmas, Michelle decorated the house and baked things that smelled good. We put up a tree. My daughters arrived with their families, and we spent a few nights sitting together telling stories about some of the good times we'd enjoyed together. We tried not to talk too much about the church or the people we'd known there.

Then, one morning, I heard a knock on the front door.

Michelle answered it.

I felt my pulse begin to race. At the time, every knock on the door sent a shiver up my spine. Even here in Vancouver, thousands of miles from the cartel, I figured some drug dealer with a gun was going to come bursting into the house and shoot me. That kind of worry doesn't just go away because you're in a place that's supposedly safe. It gnaws at you all day and all night, working its way into your bloodstream like a poison.

I ran to the front door.

In the front entryway, I found Michelle standing with her back to the visitors.

They were from the FBI.

Chapter 18

The lead agent was dressed in a black windbreaker and khakis. He looked like something out of a police procedural on television. Beside him was an older man from the Clark County Police Department. They said they'd been working together on a drug task force, and they wanted to know if I would consent to a voluntary interview.

I agreed, trying not to let the panic show on my face.

We walked through the house, now all decked out for the holidays, and sat down. One of the agents produced a folder with some pictures and notes. I got ready to defend everything I'd been doing over the past few months—the fighting, the parties with cartel guys, the tentative plans to begin running drugs for Andreas. My stomach did ten flips as the agents began talking. I got the feeling that I was done.

But as the interview went on, I got the sense that it wasn't about me.

One of the agents pulled a photo from a manila folder and placed it on the table.

"Is this your car?" he asked.

I lifted the photo and glanced at it.

There, staring at me, was Pop's old 1996 Toyota Camry. The one my mother had given to me when I was fired from the church. The one that I had rented to Greg for two hundred bucks a week.

The paint was a little chipped, and the tires looked like they'd seen better days, but I had no doubt it was the one.

"Yes," I said.

The agents explained that Greg had been arrested in downtown Vancouver while driving the car. Apparently, he'd become one of the biggest drug dealers in town—big enough to attract the attention of a joint FBI task force. The agents explained that this kind of thing happened all the time. Drug dealers tended to drive cars registered in other people's names so they wouldn't raise red flags if they got pulled over.

As they spoke, I felt a wave of guilt wash over me. At the beginning of the interview, I'd believed that this was the end of the line. It was a chance to stop the downward spiral I was in the middle of. Even an arrest would have been better than going back to Cabo and succumbing to the pressure from the cartel.

Sitting there in my kitchen, I confessed everything, even though there was, strictly speaking, nothing to confess. I hadn't broken any laws. Hanging around cartel guys wasn't a crime. Neither was getting in fights in Mexican bars or agreeing to maybe run drugs for them one day. As I spoke, the agents grew more and more distant. I kept naming sins, hoping something would stick. I told them about the affair I'd had and how I'd been fired from the church. I told them about how I'd failed my son and how he was in trouble.

The agents said they'd consider what I'd told them, and they left.

A few days later they picked me up in a van with a few other members of the task force. This was a kind of second interview. Over the next few hours, I took them around to all the drug houses I knew about, drawing on the knowledge that I'd built as the pastor of Living Hope. As we drove, I continued to make confessions, speaking in a pathetic, unending monologue about my troubles. Every time we pulled up to a drug den, I would look for David, who'd started going out again and tended to disappear for long stretches of time. If I saw him, I wanted to pull him out.

But I never saw him.

At the end of the afternoon, they dropped me off in my driveway. In a strange way, I felt like I had gotten a lot off my chest. The agents had even raised the possibility of making me an informant, which I had declined on principle. I was happy to confess to my own crimes—in fact, I *needed* to do that desperately—but I knew what happened to people who ratted on their compatriots to the feds. Not that it mattered anyway. A few days after the trip, when David was safely back home at our house in Vancouver, the FBI got in touch and let me know that they weren't interested in my services anyway.

They couldn't give me any money for the help I'd given them tracking down local dealers in Vancouver. They couldn't give me absolution for my sins either. What the FBI *could* give me, though, was my grandfather's car back. I signed some paperwork, and the agents arranged to have me come by a lot a few miles from my house and collect it.

Then they stopped calling me.

Other than a few scratches and the lingering scent of weed smoke, Pop's car was the same as it had been when I handed the keys off to Greg.

It wasn't until I got home that I popped the trunk and found the loot.

There, covered by blankets, was a couple thousand dollars' worth of stuff. Greg must have taken it as payment for drugs. I called the FBI field office right away, not wanting to be accused of profiting from drug deals. After a few minutes on hold, I got through to one of the drug task force guys and told him they'd screwed up.

"There's so much stuff in here," I said. "Watches, power tools, purses. Do you . . . like, want it back?"

The guy seemed not to know what I was talking about. Like an idiot, I pressed him on the matter, even offering to drive the car back so the agents could collect all the contraband.

"John," he said. "We don't want the stuff. Have a good day."

Finally, as I hung up the phone, I understood. It seemed that the FBI, which had heard all about my troubles (and whose agent had taken diligent notes as I unraveled in front of them), was throwing me a bone. The stuff Greg had taken in exchange for drugs was mine to keep.

For the rest of that week, I sat at my kitchen table wrapping up some of the items as Christmas gifts. My brother-in-law got a watch that was worth a few hundred bucks. My kids all got electronics. Every time I went back out to the car, I couldn't help thinking about Pop. He'd sacrificed so much of his life to make sure I didn't grow up to be a common criminal like my father, and now here I was, doling out an incarcerated drug dealer's stuff to my family like some kind of hoodrat Santa Claus.

After Christmas I sold a few of the items that were left. The money didn't amount to much, but it was more than I'd had for a long time. Over the next few days, David and I hung around the house, wondering what to do next. After all that we'd both gone through in Vancouver, there wasn't much there for us. David had no one in town who wasn't a drug dealer. If we stayed too long, I was terrified he'd take too much of something and end up dead on a couch. Neither of us liked having to drive past the half-empty storefront where Living Hope used to be. Seeing it so empty and devoid of energy broke my heart every time.

One day, David bought a new car. He pulled up to the driveway and said he was probably going to head down to Mexico.

It figures, I thought. *The only place more dangerous for him than Vancouver.*

But I'd learned enough about my son to know that he'd inherited my stubbornness. There was nothing I could do to stop him.

So I got in the car with him, and off we went.

Chapter 19

During my time in seminary, I learned about several denominations of Christianity other than my own, all the way from the early church fathers to the burgeoning religious movements in countries all over the world.

One of the strangest, to me at least, was the Calvinists. Unlike most modern Christians, these people believed in a doctrine of predestination. According to this doctrine, God had already selected all the people who were going to be saved, and you couldn't do anything to change your fate. I always thought that living that way must have been horrible—believing that your actions, if you controlled them at all, wouldn't amount to anything in the eyes of God.

But I did get a taste of what predestination must have been like as David and I drove toward Mexico. To this day, I'm convinced that no matter what we did, we still would have ended up back in Cabo, as if it was our destiny.

Driving south, we listened to Eminem on full blast. *All* of his work, from the early mixtapes all the way up to his latest releases. A few hours into the road trip, I could rap "My Name Is" back to front, with David yelling all the ad-libs like he was my hype man. I thought of all the times I'd passed by David's bedroom door in the early 2000s and heard this strange music seeping out from underneath, shaking the walls and driving Michelle and me nuts.

I could have talked to him about it then. I could have done so many things with him then, but I was too busy with my work.

When we were hungry, we'd pull into the next rest stop along the highway. I ate more McDonald's and Arby's during the five weeks we were on the road than any human being should eat in his lifetime. Somewhere in the middle of Oregon, chowing on my second Big Mac of the day, I thought my heart might actually give out from the sodium. But we'd always pull into a cheap motel, and I'd track down a little booze, and within a few hours I'd be feeling just fine again. We slept as long as we wanted to, and we got going again whenever we felt like it.

One night, in the middle of a cold snap, we checked into a hotel with a pool. A thin layer of snow covered the ground. David snorted a line of something in the room, and I downed a few beers. One of us had the bright idea to run outside and jump in the pool.

For about ten minutes, feeling the wind on our bare skin, we swam through the frigid water, sheets of ice floating past us on the pool's surface. David asked me why we'd never done this kind of thing when he was a kid. I replied that we had, recounting all the trips we'd taken in our RV, the expensive vacations to Disneyland.

"Not that," he said. "*This*."

I knew what he meant. For the past few days, we'd been talking nonstop. Whatever thoughts appeared in our heads, we'd blurt them out. I talked about my failures as a father and a pastor; he told me stories about his time in prison. Neither of us knew what we were going to do once we arrived in Cabo, and we didn't care. I had a feeling that God, even in this dark hour of debauchery and aimlessness, was pulling the strings. Later that night, as I dried myself off with a towel the size of a restaurant napkin, I prayed we'd both end up where we were supposed to be.

The next night, we pulled into a bar. We drank cheap beer and played rap songs on the jukebox. Neither of us did anything too reckless, but we ended up staying long after the place closed and talking with the staff. David went into the bathroom every few minutes, doing just enough drugs to keep himself from shaking. No one we spoke to could believe that I'd once been a pastor, which was understandable. I settled our tab with what little money we had, and we headed south, driving through the night and parking only when my vision started to get blurry.

Looking up at the signs, I realized we'd made it all the way to the Grapevine Pass in California. Head spinning, I got out of the car and walked into the nearest building, which happened to be a small bar with video poker machines against the wall. I stood at the bar and ordered the cheapest beer on the menu. David headed straight for the video poker machines, using a couple of loose coins to play whatever the game was.

A few hours later the place was nearly empty. Wind howled against the building and shook the windows in their casings. Other than the bartender, a nice old woman who seemed to have a never-ending cigarette hanging out of her mouth, David and I were the only two people in the bar. As soon as we left, the place would close.

Suddenly I heard bells and firecracker noises. David yelped. I turned around to find him standing with a white slip of paper in his hand, pointing at it like it was the winning ticket in the Mega Millions lottery.

"Dad! We just won six hundred dollars!"

Again, that wouldn't have been very much money to me a few years earlier. But now, sitting with a few crumpled dollars in my pocket and five maxed-out credit cards in my wallet, it felt like all the money in the world.

I grabbed David by the shoulders, and we jumped up and down like a couple of kids. The bartender took the cigarette out of her mouth and clapped along with us. She said she didn't have enough money in the till to cash us out but that we could stay nearby and come back the next day. After a night spent in the car using our jackets for blankets, that's what we did.

Looking back, I don't see any of this as particularly pleasant. I don't think anyone has ever *loved* sleeping in their car. But my memories of those cold nights on the road aren't entirely *un*pleasant either. When I think of the road trip I took with David, I think of the way he laughed as I told him stupid jokes. I think of the way he speed-rapped through all the verses of the songs on Eminem's *The Marshall Mathers LP 2*. I think of him looking into my eyes and finally seeing that I, his father, was there for him, willing to do anything to make him feel loved and accepted.

Do I believe that God was with us as we hit the bars and casinos we hit along the way, looking out for us as we stopped at San Francisco, Highway 1, Santa Cruz, Carmel, Santa Monica, and Oceanside? I think He was. As it says in the Bible, there's nothing on earth that happens without Him knowing. Even in the darkest moments, He's there. I believe that even as we crossed the southern border and rolled into Tijuana on fumes, God knew exactly the trouble we were headed for. He knew it would force us down into dark places and that we'd emerge from those dark places stronger than ever.

Of course, David and I didn't know that at the time. Although we both retained a strong faith in God—David had *Let Go, Let God* tattooed on his knuckles, a sentiment that was extremely important to him—we had both begun to feel like prodigals, wandering far away from the light of Christ. Even as I said my prayers and talked to locals about my faith, I was beginning to lose hope. The darkness was closing in.

And it was only going to get worse.

In Tijuana we stayed in cheap hotels, paying with some of the cash we'd won playing video poker. I got down to business. Andreas had let me know that I would need to do a few things before I could begin driving. For one thing, the cartel would need to get me a car. Then I would need to register that car in my name in the United States and apply for SENTRI, which would allow me to come and go freely over the border. The plan was for me to get all the way back down to Cabo—which was about a twenty-hour drive from Tijuana—connect with Andreas, and then travel *back* to Tijuana for meetings with the cartel.

I decided to cut out the middleman.

On the phone, Andreas was furious. He wanted to be included in the deal I made with the cartel so that he'd get a cut of whatever money I made as a driver. I promised him that I'd still give him a cut. Then I began asking about the infamous Pablo, who ran cartel business up in Tijuana. Everyone had heard his name, but no one I spoke with had ever met him in person. There were rumors that he wasn't even one guy, just a group of guys who went by a single name to avoid being caught.

Finally, Andreas agreed to set up a meeting between me and Pablo—who, he assured me, was a very real guy.

David tried to stop me.

He reminded me of what Jesus Martinez had said about the cartels. He told me stories about Americans he'd known who died after getting mixed up with the cartel. But nothing was going to stop me. At the moment, working for these guys seemed like my only option. I figured I could work within the organization, make some money, and then get out. A few hours after Andreas and I spoke on the phone, he texted to let me know that Pablo wanted to meet at a restaurant in Ensenada, Jesus's hometown.

David told me not to go. As he pleaded with me, I realized something about the road trip from Vancouver. For most people it would have taken three days, maybe four if you made a few extra stops. But David had been asking me to pull off at hotels and bars, telling me to stay a few extra days at casinos and tourist attractions. We'd been on the road for almost *five weeks*. In that time, I had felt like

David was a ten-year-old kid again, always jumping out of the car and waving me down to the next pier or tourist attraction, giggling and telling me how nice it was to be out on the road with me. And every time he could, he'd beg me not to go back to Mexico and work for the cartel.

He was dragging the trip out because he knew that as soon as I crossed the US–Mexico border, he'd lose me.

I met Pablo in a restaurant near Jesus Martinez's house. I came alone, just like he'd asked me to. Stepping into the back room, Jesus's words rang in my ears.

You always die.

But it was too late to back out. My contact had taken me all the way from Tijuana in his car, and I didn't have the money to get back on my own. I couldn't run either, given that the cartel had eyes all over the streets.

Pablo sat at a table alone and motioned for me to sit across from him. He was a middle-aged guy with nice clothes, though not so nice that he'd attract attention. Unlike Chucho, he didn't feel the need to put a gun on the table. But he was surrounded by eight bodyguards, all of whom were probably packing some serious heat.

We didn't talk business at first. Pablo asked about my life and my son. He said he'd heard good things about me. I told him about some of my earlier adventures in Mexico. The shoes. The church I'd opened. The religious missions I'd led. Something lit up in Pablo's eyes as I spoke.

"Maybe this goes well," he said, looking around the room with a big smile on his face, "and we figure out way to . . . you know, open a new church, eh? New religious mission?"

I beamed, telling him all my plans for new outreach programs. I said I'd noticed that people didn't have Christmas trees in Mexico, and I started running through my plans to harvest trees in the United States and drive them down here.

"That's great," he said. "Yes, yes. Great. We'll do that. It'll be great, Papa John."

Over the next few minutes, Pablo talked a lot of nonsense about setting me up with a new ministry. He put visions in my head of a church in Mexico that would minister to the poor. If I would just drive over the border a few times, he and the cartel would give me my old life back—or at least something better than the burnt-out, hollow life I'd been leading at the time.

Then we got down to business.

Before I could drive any product over the border, Pablo said, I would need to do a few dry runs. I'd also need a car, and Pop's old Toyota Camry wasn't going to cut it. He told me to hang around town for a few days while the cartel got things set up. I left the restaurant with a surprisingly pleasant feeling. The whole thing had felt clean and easy. It wasn't unlike signing onboarding papers for a big company.

A company that had no offboarding process.

For a few days David and I stayed with Jesus Martinez and his lovely wife in Ensenada. We made one trip to a hotel, where I met Memo, whom I remembered from my little misadventure with the shoes a few years back.

Right away I saw him eyeing David, wondering how to get him away from me. In the end, Memo slipped him a few hundred bucks and told him to go to a casino nearby. David complied, knowing how high up in the cartel Memo was. This wasn't the kind of guy you said no to.

Once Memo had me alone, he let me know how the next few days were going to go. Once my "company car," a gray Volkswagen

Passat, was ready, I would drive it to San Diego and register it in my name. Then I'd come back and wait for my SENTRI paperwork to come through. This would probably take a few weeks. Until then, my time was my own. But once the paperwork came through, I was expected to race right back here and get driving.

In the beginning, he kept up the same act that Pablo had given me in the restaurant. The cartel was going to help me build a church. They were going to arrange for the delivery of shoes and Christmas trees to the kids of the barrios. I was going to get on the right path again, and they were going to help me every step of the way.

A few days after the meeting, my car was ready. I registered it just like I was supposed to. Then it was a waiting game. At night, David and I would take Jesus Martinez out on the town, drinking beers and enjoying the nightlife in Ensenada. Jesus tried to convince me to join him in a straight business—something like selling cars or repairing fishing boats. I said I'd think about it. But I knew it was too late. I'd already accepted a car from the cartel.

The deal was done.

One afternoon I was out in Ensenada walking around, not doing much of anything, when I felt a hard bump on my right shoulder.

When I turned around, no one was there.

It wasn't until about thirty minutes later, after I'd taken a cab ride back to our hotel, that I reached into my pocket and realized my wallet had been turned inside out. In the time it had taken me to feel that single bump, a pickpocket had taken my wallet, removed everything, and slid it back in. My license was gone. So were all my credit cards.

Up in the room, I told David what had happened. He said it was common around here. Guys got so good that they could collect ten wallets in a day without the victims feeling a thing.

"There's a girl I know who can help you, though," he said. "She lives pretty close to here."

The girl turned out to be someone David had been dating on and off for a few months when he was in town. We went to see her that afternoon, and she told me she could take me to the place where the thieves tended to congregate. Under normal circumstances, I might have passed. But I needed my ID to get back and forth from Cabo to Vancouver, and I did want my credit cards back, even if they were pretty much useless at the time.

That night, the girl and I got in David's car and drove toward the spot. As we rolled through the streets of Ensenada, which grew emptier as we reached the edge of town, I studied her. She had kind eyes and a face I felt like I could trust. Her makeup was done carefully, but there was a little more of it than necessary. I thought she might have been a prostitute, although I'd later find out she wasn't.

We pulled up to a low-slung hotel with a rusted black gate in front of it. A crowd of tall women stood in the parking lot, smoking cigarettes and listening to music on a boom box. They were all decked out in the same outfit as the girl I was with, their cheap dresses glimmering in the moonlight along with their jewelry.

"Wait here," she said. "I'll go talk to them."

I put the car in Park and leaned back in the driver's seat. The girl adjusted her dress as she walked up to the black gate, knocked it open with her knee, and approached the circle of giant prostitutes. She walked up to one of the ladies and said something, shaking her finger and raising her voice. The big lady ripped her wig off and screamed.

Before I knew it, they were brawling.

The girl I'd come with punched the taller one in the stomach. Then the taller one kicked her in the shin and kneed her in the face, holding her by the hair to get another shot. Even back in the backyard fight club, I'd never seen two people go at it in such a brutal way. It was like being ringside at an MMA fight.

On instinct, I got out of the car to help the girl. I didn't have a plan. But I couldn't sit down while this lady got her ass kicked in front of me. As I approached, I began to make out a few features on the ladies in the crowd. Most of them had broad shoulders and narrow hips. Some had beer bellies. Under a layer of makeup, barely visible under the flickering streetlights above the parking lot, was facial hair.

These were dudes.

Big ones.

And as soon as they saw me, all twelve or thirteen of them started screaming and running in my direction. The girl I'd come with was already on the ground, getting pummeled by what I now understood to be a large man in a sparkly purple dress. As I watched, she hit him in the eye and managed to get him off her.

I got the sense that she did this kind of thing a lot.

I, on the other hand, did not. With almost no exceptions, I fought one guy at a time. I didn't know how to deal with a dozen angry cross-dressing prostitutes who, for reasons I didn't know, wanted to beat my ass.

One guy came at me before the others and took a swing. I ducked it and hit him in the face, walking backward to get ready for the other eleven. But I tripped on a curb and fell over, knocking my head on the pavement. I wondered as I went down how much more damage my head—which had been knocked around quite a lot over the years—could take. I got up and saw at least ten more dudes in dresses running at me, fists at the ready, screaming things in Spanish.

Up until that point, I'd prided myself on saying that I had never run from a fight in my life. No matter who wanted to take a shot at me, I'd plant my feet, raise my fists, and let them. This was especially true down in Mexico, when I had nothing left to lose.

But as Mike Tyson once said (kind of), everyone has a plan until a dozen giant men in makeup and dresses run at you like zombies.

I ran for the car, and the hookers swarmed it. It really was like being in an episode of *The Walking Dead*. I hit the gas, trying not to run anyone over, and got out right before they started breaking windows.

On the drive home, I wondered if the girl who'd shown me the place was okay. I figured she probably was. That didn't look like her first rodeo. I also marveled at just how many strange things there were to see down here in Mexico. Every time I thought I'd seen the worst one, I'd take a wrong turn and find myself confronted with something even weirder. And here in Ensenada, far from the tourist trap I'd been living in, things got *very* dark. Clearly, I wasn't in Kansas anymore.

And the trouble was just beginning.

After a few more weeks in Ensenada, David and I pressed on, joined by Jesus. Mrs. Martinez had clearly had enough of us hanging around. In the bottom of my backpack, I managed to find a small piece of gold that turned out to be worth a few hundred dollars. David and I split the money with Jesus Martinez, who I knew would use it to get us down to Cabo rather than blowing it gambling. It felt like God was providing for us, just as He had provided for Elijah during his rebellion. Some nights, we slept in our car. Somehow we managed to roll into Cabo San Lucas together on fumes, pulling into the driveway of our vacation house in the middle of the night. It was strange, having a vacation house and not being able to afford gas. But that's where we were.

Getting there felt good. But it also made me nervous. Although I hadn't realized it at the time, I had probably chosen to *drive* all the way down to Mexico with David because it was the slowest way I knew to travel. While David was trying to prolong the road trip to save me, I was doing the same thing to save him. In part, I think I chose to go to Cabo because I knew that for all its seedy aspects, the one drug you couldn't do there was heroin. The leader of the local cartel had lost a family member to the drug, and anyone who sold it in his jurisdiction was killed. I figured if David had any chance of avoiding the drug to which he'd become so addicted, it was in Cabo.

In reality, though, nothing waited for him out there but danger—and probably death. It didn't matter whether we were in Washington or Mexico or Alaska. Until David got a handle on his demons, he wasn't going to be safe out in the world. As a father, that pained me to my core. But there was only so much I could do to help him, especially when I was dealing with so many demons of my own.

Sure enough, a few days after we arrived in Cabo, I got a call in the middle of the night telling me that David had been in a car wreck. I figured he was dead for sure. But when I arrived at the scene, an empty road just outside of town, I was relieved to find him awake. One of his legs was pretty messed up, but other than that he'd escaped unscathed. All around us, Mexican cops spoke to one another and looked at slips of paper.

That gave me a bad feeling.

Over the years, I'd heard about what happens to Americans who get mixed up with the Mexican authorities. My suspicions were confirmed when a guy in a uniform came over to David and started filling him in on what had happened. As it turned out, the man whose car he'd hit was a surgeon with an ownership stake in a nearby hospital.

The same hospital they ended up taking him to.

I followed close behind the ambulance that was transporting David, then followed him into the hospital and waited while they got him a bed. A nurse put a catheter in him, and doctors milled around, planning to test his blood alcohol content. Watching it all happen, I made a quick decision that I needed to get David out of this place. I removed the catheter myself, trying to ignore my son's screams of pain, and carried him out to my car when no one was looking. We drove away, hoping we'd seen the last of the trouble, knowing all the while that we probably hadn't.

As soon as we got home, Jesus Martinez and I went to the impound lot where they'd put David's car and broke into it. Up in a secret compartment in the roof, I found some drugs and a few hundred dollars in cash. I took it all so they wouldn't be able to pin charges on him. Little did I know that they didn't need any evidence.

A few weeks later, Mexican cops showed up at the house with an arrest warrant. But David's name was spelled wrong, and they wouldn't specify charges. I managed to make them go away, but I had a feeling that, like all cartel-connected people in Cabo, they'd be back soon. Until then, I'd stay with my son and protect him however I could.

When the text message from the cartel came, there was nothing I could do. My SENTRI paperwork had come through, and it was time for me to begin driving. Memo texted and told me to get back to Tijuana.

It was time.

Chapter 20

The next day, I met Memo in the lobby of my hotel. He looked like he'd aged two decades in the weeks since I'd seen him.

Cartel life, as I would soon learn, will do that to you.

At first glance, he looked like any other middle-aged guy coming through Tijuana on business. He wore button-down shirts and nice jeans, a watch that was nice enough when you looked at it but not so nice that you noticed it right away. I might have missed him if he hadn't approached me first.

"Papa John?"

"Yeah."

"Memo."

From there, we were off.

Memo explained that it would take a few days to get everything set up. Until then, I would stay in a hotel room upstairs, and another guy from the cartel would stay with me. When I asked why, Memo laughed.

"To make sure you don't run," he said.

It was my first indication that as far as the cartel was concerned, I was not an employee. I was property.

I checked into my hotel room and met my new roommate, a quiet guy with tattoos all over his body who'd found himself in debt to the cartel. He didn't say why, and I didn't ask. Sitting down in a chair near the window, I flicked on the television and watched a Mexican sitcom, trying to keep track of the quick Spanish dialogue. In all the time I'd been coming down to Mexico, I'd never bothered to fully learn the language. I'd always found I could get by smashing my broken Spanish against everyone's broken English.

Now that I'd become a virtual prisoner of the Sinaloa drug cartel, my inability to understand the language was beginning to seem like a big obstacle. Every day, guys threw Spanish phrases over my head too quickly for me to grasp them. I'm sure a few of my handlers thought I was a little slow mentally. I mean, what were they supposed to think when some fat white guy came around telling stories in bad Spanish about all the souls he'd saved and the religious missions he'd done, going on and on about God and how to live a good life, while he was waiting to smuggle drugs for a criminal organization? I must have sounded out of my mind.

I set off early the next morning and headed for the border. There were no drugs in the car. This was a dry run, and I'd be making quite a few of them over the next few days. Traffic on the way up was brutal, as it usually was. Up ahead, I saw the familiar signs and guard towers. Agents stood atop each one, their binoculars gleaming in the morning sunlight. Some of these guys, I knew, were on the cartel payroll. They'd send information about which guards would be stationed where, and wave friendly cars into the right lanes with secret signals. As strange as it might sound, this made me feel secure, as if a big organization was looking after me, and I was just a small cog, driving my car.

I got through without a problem. Then I turned around and came back.

The next day, I did it again.

And again.

And again, and again, and again.

Whenever I wasn't driving, I would stay in my hotel room watching Mexican TV. I was allowed to leave for just under an hour every night to pick up food at the only restaurant nearby, which was KFC.

I felt greasy and fat. Other than walking to and from my car, I wasn't getting any exercise. The hotel room was small and dark, and the rotating cast of guys I had to share it with gave me a strange feeling of being in a dream. There was always a guy in the room with me who didn't speak my language, and he always had a look on his face like he'd screwed up royally.

I knew the feeling.

I drank beer. I watched TV. I ate fried chicken. I drove. Then I drank some more beer and ate some more chicken and drove. I watched TV. I ate fried chicken. I drove. I drank beer. I yearned for a little action. Anything to break the monotony.

Then, one night, walking to the KFC, I got some.

The van came out of nowhere and cornered me. Four guys jumped out.

I was against the wall. The guys came up close and spoke in broken English.

"You work for Memo," one said. "Work for us instead. Better pay. No shit hotels. Come work for us. Let's go."

I got the sense right away that they were from a rival cartel. But I didn't know which one. I didn't know anything else about them. To me, they looked similar to all the other cartel-affiliated thugs who'd cornered me looking for money or work. It was getting exhausting.

But at least it was a change of pace.

We talked for a few minutes. I told them my life story, and they asked what I was getting paid by Memo's guys. I told them. They said they'd offer me more. I hemmed and hawed, trying to steer the conversation away.

Behind them a car pulled up, and they turned to look at it.

Memo got out of the driver's side with a gun in his hand. He pointed it at the guys and grabbed me by the shirt, pulling me back into the car.

We drove away in silence.

After a while I told him I was getting bored. The isolation was getting to me, and my money was running out.

"Don't worry," he said. "Tomorrow, we do the real thing."

Chapter 21

The next morning, Memo knocked on my door with a younger guy.

"Your handler," he said.

Together, the two of us drove toward the border and pulled off at an exit about a half mile from the San Ysidro checkpoint.

There, waiting for me in the low light of the rising sun, was my gray Volkswagen Passat, filled with drugs.

Out of curiosity, I asked how they'd managed to stuff the weed into the car. I couldn't see anything different about it, and the new car smell still clung to the interior. Nothing seemed amiss, which was good.

"There," said the handler, pointing at the back bumper. "And there, and there, and there."

He pointed to the front bumper, the bottom of the car, and the space behind the stereo system. Every square inch of free space, it seemed, had been stuffed with product. When I got in and tried to turn on the stereo, I realized it wasn't working.

"Gone," said the handler. "All gone. Hollow."

I nodded and put the car in Drive. The handler handed me a burner phone and told me to wait for a text once I got over the border.

"We'll give you instructions," he said.

From there, the drive was normal. I drove through the heavy traffic in front of the checkpoint and pulled up to the front of the

SENTRI lane. When the border guard asked for my ID, I handed it over. I was a pastor heading to church. A guy in front waved me through, and I drove up the highway into the United States of America.

I exhaled, surprised how easy it had been. After a few miles the burner phone blinked with a text.

805N to Denny's.

I pulled off at the exit and parked in front of the restaurant. They'd told me to leave the keys in the ignition, so I did. Then I went in and sat at the counter, trying not to turn around every ten seconds to make sure the car was still there.

I ordered eggs, looking around.

It was amazing, I thought, how little Denny's had changed over the years. The tables were the same. The carpets were the same. Even the layout was the same. Looking over at the corner, I could almost see myself and Michelle sitting over empty plates of food on our first date, talking for hours while the waitresses hovered, wanting us to go home. I missed how simple our lives had been then. I wanted to go back and make different decisions—to take her hand and leave the restaurant and go somewhere far away from Vancouver. But even then, I had the feeling that I still would have ended up here, shoveling the first non-KFC food I'd had in weeks into my mouth, waiting for a couple of thugs to come collect my drugs so I could make some money.

Still, I believed God was leading me to something. I just didn't know what.

An hour passed.

I turned around and the car was gone.

I ordered coffee and stared straight ahead, trying not to attract too much attention.

I don't know how long it was before the car appeared again. Two hours, maybe three. All I know is that I turned around to check, pretending I was stretching my neck, and there was the car, emptied of product, parked in the same spot.

I waited for a text telling me what to do. But nothing came. I walked out to the parking lot and got in the car, then drove back across the border.

Back to the hotel, to monotony and fried chicken and sitcoms whose jokes I couldn't understand.

Memo was waiting in the parking lot when I pulled up. He asked how things had gone, and I said fine.

"Good," he said. "Because you're going again tomorrow."

From then on, I drove most days. The routine was the same. My handler would take me to the car, and I'd drive it across. I'd sit for a while in a restaurant—sometimes Denny's, sometimes Arby's, sometimes a diner with Mexican beer on tap—and chat with the waitstaff at the counter while the guys on the US side of the cartel operation retrieved the product.

The reason I could get into the US without trouble, I learned, is that border patrol believed I was a commuter. That meant I had to cross the border on a regular basis, or they'd begin to suspect my cover story was fake. So my full-time job became making runs for the cartel. Once I'd gone five times, I got paid a few thousand dollars—more money than I had seen in a long time.

One of the first things I did was call Michelle, who'd moved to Yuma, Arizona, to be close to her father. He'd been sick for a while, and things had taken a bad turn recently. I told her things were good in Mexico and that I'd gotten a job selling cars. I paid my family's bills, happy to be providing again.

At night I would sit on the balcony of my hotel and call Jesus

Martinez, who'd come to feel like my only friend in the world. We'd talk about his business, and he'd ask about my new life with the cartel. Whenever I paused for more than a few seconds, he'd remind me of the danger I was getting into. Sometimes he'd tell me to get back into legit business. That would involve some interaction with the cartel but not the kind that tends to get people killed. I'd refuse every time. There was something about the cartel lifestyle I was beginning to like.

By then I was the unofficial spiritual leader for the whole cartel. I'd hang out with the guys until four thirty in the morning. We'd drink beer and I'd give them a few of the Adderall pills I'd been prescribed back in Vancouver for my ADHD. For some reason, the guys liked these pills even better than straight meth. One night, one of them cornered me to make sure I wasn't selling them to anyone else.

"If you do," he said, "then we have a *big* problem, Papa John."

"No, no, no," I told him, telling the truth. "I bring them for you guys. You guys like them. Right?"

"Good."

Late at night, hopped up on booze and Adderall, the guys would confess everything to me: the guilt they felt about always cheating on their wives, the bad dreams they had about all the people they'd had to kill. I'd always listen, trying to imagine what that kind of life was like. By the end of the night, I'd usually have brought at least one of the men to Christ. Hearing the message from me rather than a priest made it more palatable.

I felt like a pastor again.

One night, at a pig roast for a bunch of sicarios in town, I asked why the cartel kept me around. Surely there were other white guys who could drive stuff over the border for them, and those other white guys didn't come with all the baggage I did.

"Honestly, Papa John, we have no idea," said one guy, chomping on his roast pig with a pistol beside his plate. "It's just like . . . *no one* knows what your deal is. You're just here! And you're fun!

It's like, is he a *padre*? Is he a crazy fighter? What's going on with this crazy guy? *That's* why."

It wasn't a great answer, but I got it. I couldn't deny I was a good time.

But as I watched people ruin their lives in the drug trade, I did begin to have my doubts about the long-term viability of this career, if you could even call it that. By the third or fourth time I asked about a friend of mine only to learn that he'd been shot dead in the streets, I'd had my fill of driving for the cartels. Around the summertime, when the farmers down in Sinaloa stop growing so much weed, I pulled Memo aside and told him I probably wasn't going to come back and drive for him.

"I just need a break, man," I said. "I'm thinking about going into business with a friend. Thanks for the opportunity and all, but . . . I don't know, I think I'm done."

He wasn't happy, but he seemed to take it all in stride. I wasn't sure if I'd made a mistake. After all, there was no HR department at the Sinaloa Cartel for me to talk to about giving two weeks' notice or receiving a severance package. There was no recourse to any authority other than Memo, and Memo could be unpredictable: coked up and rageful one second and goofy the next. I left the bar that night with a bad feeling. Something else Jesus Martinez had once told me echoed in my ears as I walked along the streets.

They don't just let you go, John. It doesn't work like that.

A few days later I got a phone call.

David, who'd been staying with me at the house on and off, was sitting in a Mexican police station.

He'd been arrested.

The next few weeks were a blur.

I drove to see David, getting disturbing flashbacks of the

mornings I used to spend visiting him in prison up in Forks, which at the time had seemed like the most dangerous place for him to be. Now my son was locked up in a building in a foreign country with guys who made US inmates look like Martha Stewart. I knew because I had known many of them on the outside. They were killers, rapists, and drug lords with rap sheets longer than Russian novels. And there was nothing they hated more than short white people who came into town and got mixed up in their system.

No matter how many people I asked, no matter how hard I pounded my fist on the table or tried to charm the lady at the front desk of the prison, no one would tell me what charges my son had been arrested on. Whenever I pressed them, they laughed, as if I didn't know how things worked down here.

In Mexico the state police are the military arm of the cartel. Nothing more. It's not uncommon in that country to hear that a local politician—or even a national one—has been assassinated in broad daylight because the cartel no longer wanted them in power. And the people who aren't important enough to assassinate, they arrest, knowing that the prison system will probably kill them anyway.

I had crossed the cartel, and the cartel had retaliated.

By locking up my son.

I left the prison in a daze, the guilt building in my chest. I'd rushed into a deal with the devil, and now I was paying the price. Nothing happened in this town without the cartel knowing about it. I drove to the United States consulate, waiting hours to speak with someone. No one could help me. I called every dirty cop and cartel guy I knew, trying to get some information. None of them would talk either.

After a few days of brooding and worrying, I drove out to a taco stand in San Jose Del Cabo and met with the head of a rival cartel. I wanted to know if there was anything I could do to help my son while he was in prison.

"There's one thing," he said. "If you're prepared to pay."

Chapter 22

The gates of the Mexican state prison creaked open. I could hear music blasting from cheap stereos and phrases shouted in Spanish. A guard led me through the front walkway and into the building, with its peeling paint and empty, echoey hallways. As I looked around, I noticed that the sounds were dying.

"Where are we going?" I asked.

"Villa's wing," he said.

At this prison, he explained, Villa was a big dog. And big dogs needed space. Across the yard, more than a hundred prisoners, my son included, were jammed into their blocks like sardines, sometimes four or five to a cell. Villa, on the other hand, lived alone in his own wing of the prison with four bodyguards. He ate whatever he wanted. The guards were on his payroll.

Everyone, even the cops, was scared shitless to cross him.

In another life, Villa had been a sicario: a hit man for the New Generation Cartel, just like my old pal Chucho. Only this guy was in a different league. Over a thirty-year career, beginning when he was only a kid, Villa had racked up 350 confirmed kills. That was enough bodies to fill all the cells in his wing of the prison and then some. If my brain hadn't been occupied by other things at the time, I might have wondered what it was like to walk around with that much blood on your hands—with that many memories of pointing guns at people and pulling the trigger, wiping them off the face of the earth for good.

Needless to say, I wasn't going to try asking the guy what he thought about God. We didn't have that kind of time.

All I cared about was securing protection for David. At the moment, he was a small white guy in prison with hundreds of Mexicans, and he'd made plenty of enemies during his time in the country. Although he'd been blessed with his father's confidence, he didn't have the muscle and fuck-you attitude to back it up. Without someone looking out for him on the inside, I knew he'd be dead in a matter of hours.

I hustled up the hallway toward a small room, willing to trade away anything if it meant safety for my son.

Villa, dressed in a white undershirt and orange prison-issue pants, walked in. He was tall, but not too tall. Mean, but not too mean. Like all the other most dangerous people I knew, you wouldn't think twice if you passed him on the street.

Which, I thought, *is probably why he's been able to kill so many people. They never see him coming.*

Villa sat and asked how I was doing. I told him the truth, which was, "Not great."

"Your son?" he said, getting right to the point.

"Yes. I need protection for him."

Villa leaned back in his chair, sensing he had the upper hand. But he didn't ask me for anything.

"You're Papa John, yes? The padre?"

"I am, yeah. But I really need—"

He cut me off and asked another question. I was so stressed out that I don't remember what it was. But I do remember that by the end of the meeting, Villa had put me at ease. We talked about my ministry and my fall from grace, all the people we knew. I told him I'd been driving for the cartel down in Cabo and that I was making good money doing it.

By the end of our time together, he was smiling.

"Your son will be protected," he said. "You have my word. In here, he'll be one of my guys. And no one touches my guys."

Looking at him, I believed it.

"I hate to ask, man, but . . ."

"What do you owe me?" he said, finishing the question.

"Yeah."

"We'll figure it out. Later."

I left the prison with a sense of foreboding building in my stomach. On the way out, I heard the hollering out in the yard. The sounds of rusty barbells dropping made me jump. Any one of those sounds could have been a gunshot or a riot alarm. At any moment I could get the call that David had been killed. I had no idea what it meant to owe a favor to someone like Villa. I knew nothing was off the table.

Out of the corner of my eye, I also saw men unloading boxes. Something about them didn't look quite right.

But I knew David was safe.

And that was all I could hope for right then.

Late that summer I was still living in my house in Cabo, but I found I could wander around a little more freely, despite the fact that Memo was calling me at least three times a day.

Around that time, I also started getting messages on WhatsApp—the preferred messaging service of criminals everywhere—from guys who said they were friends with Villa. They were just quick check-ins at first, asking me how things were going, seeing if I needed anything. Once or twice, I met some guys for beer at local spots they knew, and we got along well.

One night, after we'd had a few, I asked how Villa was doing in prison, and one of his buddies got a funny look in his eye.

"Really well," he said.

I kept visiting David whenever I could, loading up his commissary account with money so he could buy things to trade: cigarettes, bags of candy. Michelle called often to ask me how things were going. I'd always lie to her. I found myself working hard to make up stories about all the fake cars I'd sold that month. For a while I told her it was Volkswagens (easy to remember since I smuggled drugs in one every day), and then I switched to Fords and Chevys. During one of Michelle's rare trips down to Mexico, I even made arrangements with a friend who owned a car dealership to let us come in and walk around, pretending I worked there. For a while, I worked as hard at lying to my wife as I'd once worked at some of the businesses I had built.

Then one morning, I got a call. The voice on the other end was familiar, but I couldn't tell why.

"Is this Papa John?" it said.

The voice got serious, falling almost to a whisper.

"I'm a nurse," it said. "At the prison hospital. We have your son here, and it's . . . well, it's bad."

I froze and fell backward onto the couch, pressing the phone to my ear. There were sirens in the background.

The ones that go off when there's a riot.

"What happened?"

"He says . . . well, he says he fell off a bed. But I don't think that's what happened. You should get here."

I was out the door before he could finish the sentence, running out to the driveway to get my car. Before I knew it, I was halfway to the hospital, driving so fast that the world outside became a blur. If I hit anything at this speed, I'd be squished like a grape.

I parked at the hospital and ran upstairs, thinking of that day all those years ago when I'd been kicked in the nose and rushed to the hospital in Vancouver. That night it was four-year-old David sitting at the foot of my bed, wondering whether he was ever going to see his daddy again. Tonight the roles were reversed. I entered the hospital room, paid off the nurse (who wasn't supposed to allow visitors into the room), and stood at the end of David's bed. His foot was mangled almost beyond recognition, bruised and misshapen like a purple sack full of sheet metal.

"It's called 'stomping,'" said the nurse. "The guys in prison know how to do it. They come up to a man in the yard, stomp in just the right place on the foot, and break every bone. If it's not treated, the person never walks again. They drag it, like a . . . like a . . ."

"Clubfoot," I said.

"Yes, that."

No matter how many times I asked David what had happened, he still said he'd fallen out of his bed. But unless he'd fallen into a running wood chipper, I wasn't buying it. This was calculated.

"What about Villa?" I asked the nurse. "We had . . . an arrangement."

The guy stopped what he was doing and put down his clipboard.

"You haven't heard?" he said.

I asked what he was talking about.

"I mean, turn on the news, Papa John. It's everywhere."

Long story short: Villa had finally pulled off an escape he'd been planning since he got locked up, and he'd done it just a few hours before David got his foot stomped on. For months, Villa's associates—some of whom were prison guards—had been sneaking tiny pieces of guns into the prison. A magazine here, a barrel there, some bullets hidden in cardboard boxes. Early that morning, Villa and a few other guys had put the pieces together, loaded up the guns, and marched out of the prison before sunrise.

And the protective bubble they'd been providing my son went with them.

I sat up with David all night, not moving from his bedside. Unlike that night all those years earlier, I had no doubt he'd survive his injuries. But I didn't know what would happen to him when he went back into the prison. Clearly the foot stomp was a warning. Sitting there in my hard chair, trying to keep my composure, I realized that warning hadn't been for David.

It had been for me.

"I'll do it," I told Memo. "I'll come back. I'll drive."

I was outside David's room on my cell phone, trying to keep my voice down.

"Good," Memo said.

"But I have conditions," I said, fully aware that I wasn't in a very good negotiating position.

Memo paused. I decided to keep going.

"I need David out of prison. *Now.* And when he gets out, I need one day with him before I come back and work for you. Just one day."

Again, there was silence on the other end of the line.

"Fine," he said. "One day."

I hung up the phone, my suspicions confirmed. I hadn't said a word about the assault. Memo, or someone who worked for him, had probably orchestrated the whole thing.

Three days later, I stood behind David in a Mexican courtroom, listening to a judge rattle on in Spanish. No one seemed sure of what the charges against him were. But the way they looked at his wrecked foot told me they knew it involved the cartel. There was no longer any doubt in my mind that Memo would go after anyone in my family to force me back into driving.

Within a few hours, David and I were in the car headed back to our house. He'd been cleared of all charges by the judge. Michelle came down, and we took David to a doctor, who let us know that he'd need to have surgery on his foot if he ever wanted to walk normally again. Michelle almost collapsed when he said the surgery would cost about $5,000. She turned to me, wondering if I could come up with that kind of cash. For the first time, I got the feeling that she might have known I'd been lying to her. But she didn't say anything.

I told the doctor I'd come up with the money, and we took

David home. A girl he'd been seeing named Arisbeth came with us. We barbecued steaks in the backyard and sat around an outdoor table as a family, trying to forget the nightmare we were all in the middle of. Michelle didn't speak to me much. She spent most of her time tending to David, who was still in a great deal of pain. We surprised him by bringing out a new puppy we'd bought for him that weekend, and he named it Booger, calling it Boogie for short.

Before I knew it, the sun was setting and my one day of freedom had ended. Memo texted me that night with instructions on which flophouse hotel in Tijuana I was supposed to report back to.

It was time to drive again.

Chapter 23

For me, Tijuana was the loneliest place on earth. I'd spend most of my time in run-down hotel rooms, talking with Jesus Martinez on the phone, not wanting to bother Michelle too often. She was down in Cabo, sitting with David while he waited for his surgery. Although she was shaken, to put it mildly, she was glad she could be there for David when he needed his mom.

I, on the other hand, had no friends. Sure, there were people around me all the time, several of whom saw me as a spiritual leader or a therapist. But there's an old saying about friends: If they'd shoot you and bury you in the desert at the first sign of trouble, they're not *really* your friends. (At least I think that's a saying; if not, it should be.) My only real contact with the outside world came through WhatsApp, which was always filled with messages from Villa's friends asking me to come out for beer and pizza.

I knew they were dangerous guys, but I'd always had a good time with them. We'd sit around talking about our families and our friends; they'd always be interested in what I had to say. They laughed at my jokes and picked up my tab. I knew they were all affiliated with Jalisco New Generation, a rival cartel. But I didn't think hanging with them at restaurants was something that could get me killed. It wasn't like I got a handy cartel handbook on my first day of driving that had all the rules and regulations inside. All I knew was that I was finally getting a little human connection.

Soon Villa reached out personally. He didn't say where he was or how he'd managed to escape. He didn't even mention that big favor I owed him for protecting David in prison. All he wanted was a few minutes of my time.

"Go meet a friend of mine," he said. "At the dog track."

A few hours later I was in the stands of Caliente Stadium in Tijuana, watching skinny greyhounds chase a rabbit around a track. Cheers erupted from the spectators at the end of each race. Every few minutes, a guy would leave with his head in his hands, having lost everything on a bad bet.

Been there, I thought.

I placed a few bets and drank beer. The guy Villa had told me to look for hadn't shown up yet. Looking across the track at the property's big casino, I thought of all the nights I'd spent with David on the road, staying in free hotel rooms and gambling with the last few dollars we had to our name. I felt a pang of guilt that my actions had put him in prison.

Then the sun darkened, and I heard a voice from behind me.

"Papa John?"

I turned to find the biggest Mexican I'd ever seen in my life. The guy, whose name was Gordo, looked like he could pick me up, fold me in two, and stuff me in his pocket. Shaking his hand was like grabbing a bunch of bananas.

I told him who I was. He explained he was Villa's friend. For the next few hours, as we watched the races and sat at the bar having drinks, I waited for him to call in Villa's favor. I prepared a dozen different ways to refuse, most of which involved invoking my employment with the Sinaloa Cartel. But the question never came. We just sat there for hours, talking about our lives. I cracked a few jokes in Spanish, which still wasn't great, and Gordo cracked up at all of them. When the sun went down, he texted a few other people and had them come meet us.

"There's a girl coming," he said. "I think you'll like her."

A few minutes later Sonya showed up. She was young and pretty. Her hair was bright red, and her English was better than that of most Mexican girls. I could tell right away that something about her was off. For one thing, she seemed very interested in talking to me, and I had given her zero indication that I felt the same way. Every time I brushed her off, she'd come right back, getting close to me, asking about my job with the cartel, offering to fill up my drink when it was only half empty.

"I just got out of prison," she said. "Drug running. I'm trying to turn over a new leaf."

I gave her some advice about leaving a life of crime behind, not stopping for one second to consider the irony. To these people, I was a spiritual leader. The world was upside down. I was drinking Mexican beer by the gallon, and my thoughts were spilling out of my mouth like vomit. I couldn't stop myself from talking.

As the night wore on, I started venting to Sonya about my frustrations with working for the Sinaloa guys. Gordo listened from across the bar, keeping an eye on us both to make sure we were getting along.

"They've got me in these cheap hotels," I found myself saying. "I keep asking to get out, but they say I can't. I'm looking for a new place. Something nicer."

From there, the night was a blur. All I know is that nothing happened between me and Sonya. She'd done what she came there to do, which was to get me talking. The next morning, I woke up to a bunch of texts from Gordo asking if I was still interested in moving into one of their apartments.

Why not? I figured. *We're all friends.*

A few days later Sonya picked me up at my hotel with Gordo. I got in the back of the car with all my belongings in one suitcase.

In the days since our first meeting at the dog track, Villa's friends had offered to put me up at a nicer place near his own house. It was a gated community with eight buildings, most of which were still in the process of being built. Driving up, I noticed a shiny McMansion next to the gate with kids playing in the yard. I figured the rest of the community would include similarly well-appointed homes.

I was wrong.

As soon as Gordo opened the door, I could tell something wasn't right. The walls of my new apartment were unpainted. Every surface smelled like sawdust. Out the window, I saw a garage across the street filled with Mexican guys working with wood and carrying sheetrock around the complex. A few guys stood off to one side cleaning guns with dirty rags. Strange men of all skin tones walked around, looking like prisoners who didn't know what they were in for.

Every few seconds the sound of a chop saw rang out, making me jump.

Sonya asked what I thought of the place, and I said it was great, trying to be nice. Gordo took a seat at a rickety table and removed his pistol from its holster. I hadn't noticed it before. We talked for a few minutes, trying to keep up the energy of our first meeting at the dog track. Then Sonya walked over to the window, wiped some dust off the glass, and pointed outside.

"See that guy?" she said.

I walked over and looked. There, parked in the middle of the empty street, was a white Ford Taurus. A thin Chinese guy leaned against it smoking a cigarette.

"Yeah."

"You're going to drive him across the border for us," Sonya said.

When I looked back at her, she was all business. The kind, goofy girl from the dog track was gone. Gordo sat at the table, eyes forward. Construction dust hung in the air between us, visible in the harsh light of the midday sun.

"No, Sonya," I said. "I'm not."

She furrowed her eyebrows and stepped closer to me, lowering her voice. "Are you fucking serious right now?"

I did a quick calculation in my head. Running weed over the border was one thing; I knew the price of getting caught (or, at least, I *thought* I knew the price of getting caught). Running *people* over the border opened me up to a whole bunch of charges I hadn't even considered. Smuggling. Kidnapping. Probably some other things that tended to land people like me on *America's Most Wanted*.

I told Sonya yes, I was serious.

She said, "Don't you owe Villa a favor?"

I froze. The rickety walls of the apartment seemed to fall around me. My stomach dropped. All this time, I had thought I was making friends. I had actually come to believe that the favor I owed Villa was all in the past. Now I was locked in a shitty apartment complex—which, I realized as I looked around, seemed to be some kind of safe house for human traffickers from China—being forced at gunpoint to drive human beings over the border. I looked back at Gordo, who seemed to be tracking my every move. His gun was still on the table. One false move, and it would be pointed at the center of my forehead.

I tried to explain, telling Sonya that I couldn't drive in a car that wasn't registered to me. I told her what might happen if I got pulled over driving a car that was in someone else's name. I told her I was afraid to get popped for kidnapping. I told her I was already working for the Sinaloa Cartel, and I couldn't just start working for another organization without clearing it with my bosses first.

"Well, what are you smuggling for them?" she asked.

"Weed."

"Oh!" she said, brightening. "This is different! This is smuggling *people*. It's a completely different thing. They won't mind."

Now, I was a moron back then. I didn't know the rules. But even *I* could sense that this was bullshit. I thought of Jesus's warning about people who get involved with the cartel. I thought of Memo and the way he'd pulled up that night with a gun in his hand to stop me from even talking to people from rival cartels.

Still, the gun was on the table. And I couldn't outthink a gun. I also wasn't going to get in a fight with a girl, no matter how much of a badass she was.

I stood quietly, pretending to think it over. Sonya glared at me the whole time. Finally I said I would do it, asking for a few details about the run. Sonya filled me in. We'd leave first thing in the morning, and the New Generation Cartel would guide me the whole way. I'd be driving the Chinese guy outside, plus a few other people, who'd be arriving shortly. I nodded, and the friendly atmosphere returned to the room.

"You know, we're still going to pay you," Sonya said. "You're not like our *prisoner* or anything. Like, what do you make driving for the boys from Cabo?"

"About three grand," I told her.

"We can double that, John," she said. "Seven thousand every time you bring people over. This business is *very* lucrative. And it's totally different from drugs. All good!"

I nodded, trying to buy time.

Sonya left in the late afternoon, telling me to rest up. But Gordo stayed, taking his gun out every few minutes and cradling it in his massive hands, as if to remind me it was still there.

I walked into my bedroom, where a dust-covered mattress lay in the middle of a shiny hardwood floor. Gordo followed, his massive body casting a long shadow over me. I looked around at the half-finished room and thought about the men across the street cleaning guns. I pictured the guy leaning against the car, feeling like Denzel Washington in *The Equalizer*. No matter what happened, this wasn't going to be good.

I had two choices.

Either I could take my chances and drive these people over the border, opening myself up to charges of smuggling and kidnapping and God only knew what else.

Or I could run.

Standing there with my hands at my sides, pretending I was getting ready for a nap, I made my decision.

I stretched out and turned to Gordo, acting like I'd just remembered something.

"You know what," I said, "I forgot I said I'd call my wife. Be right back."

I walked out the front door and hung around on the porch, waiting for him to follow me. But he didn't. About fifty yards up ahead, the rickety gate swung open on wheels to make way for a black SUV that had just arrived. I looked down at my flip-flops, wondering if I should kick them off.

Before I could decide one way or the other, I looked down again and found I was already running.

Years earlier, when I was still the lead pastor of Living Hope, I used to tell people that preaching seven weekend services—especially the way *I* preached them—was like running at top speed for an hour.

Sprinting past a garage full of cartel members in my ragged flip-flops, trying to look like I wasn't running away from their boss's boss, I realized I was probably wrong about that. Sprinting at top speed was *much* harder than preaching.

My heart pounded right away. A stabbing pain hit me right in the lungs. My knees, both of which had been replaced years ago, clanked against my leg bones, sending waves of pain all through my body.

And I hadn't even made it to the gate yet.

Behind me someone yelled in Spanish. I didn't know what

they were saying, but it didn't sound like *Go ahead, John, no hard feelings!*

I reached the gate, which was almost closed, and slipped out.

The road was paved, but there was nowhere to hide. I kept running. The gate creaked open again behind me, and I heard a car engine revving. That kicked me into a higher gear, and I ran even faster. I felt like I was going to puke.

As I ran, buildings appeared. Small houses and tiny stores set back a little from the road. In Tijuana these were called "nowhere stores." I thought about running inside, ducking behind the counter, and waiting for a few hours. But I had no way of knowing that the store owners didn't work for the cartel.

Night was approaching. I slowed to a light jog and hid in a bush when my legs gave out. Cars sped up the road every few minutes.

Any one of them, I knew, could be Gordo or Sonya.

Or Villa himself, who'd be more than happy to add some idiot gringo like me to his list of confirmed kills.

I took out my phone on instinct and dialed the only person who could help me.

Who, I realized as the phone began to ring, might want to kill me more than anyone right now.

Memo pulled up about an hour later in a nice car.

I'd told him almost everything over the phone, although I'm not sure he heard me over the sound of his own screaming and cursing.

He'd called me an idiot. He'd threatened to leave me out in the street to die. But he'd calmed down eventually, happy that I was talking to him again, and told me to wait under the nearest street sign.

I was quiet as I pulled myself into the car, rubbing my aching knees and trying to explain to him how I'd ended up at a rival cartel's safe house. I told him I was tired of living in cheap hotels and that I needed something more stable if I was going to keep working for him. Sitting in the passenger seat with my hair all messed up and my Hawaiian shirt reeking of sweat, I probably looked like the most pathetic human being on the planet. Even Memo, who, if I haven't made it clear by now, was not the most empathetic man in the world, took some pity on me.

"I get it," he said. "If I got you a long-term place, would that help? Like, one of my rentals?"

I said it would.

We drove in silence for a mile or two, nearing the compound I'd just run away from. From the front seat of Memo's car, watching the last rays of sunlight sink under the horizon line in the distance, the whole thing began to seem like a dream. Maybe it hadn't even been as dangerous as I'd thought while I was in the middle of it.

"Hey," I said to Memo, breaking the silence that had come over the car. "I hate to ask another favor. But I left my suitcase back there. Do you think they'd be cool with us swinging by to get it?"

He laughed.

Then he stopped to catch his breath and laughed some more.

Finally I said, "What?"

"You're kidding," he said.

I told him I wasn't.

"Dude," he said, finally coughing out the last of the giggles. "Do you understand what you just did? We *kill* people for that. You don't work for two rival cartels. When I get you a house, which I will, it's going to have to be in a secret location."

"Why?"

"Because they're going to be looking for you."

For the rest of the ride, I didn't say a word.

Chapter 24

Later that fall Memo made good on his promise and found me a day-to-day rental in a neighborhood not far from the border. It wasn't luxurious or anything, but I didn't have to step over piles of construction dust on my way to the kitchen table for breakfast. It was also free of strange men with guns (at least that I could see), which was nice.

Every time I stepped outside, I'd look around, expecting someone to come and put a few bullets in my face. I thought often about Chucho, the man I'd prayed over in the desert. One moment he'd been walking tall, scaring the crap out of people like he was king of the neighborhood. The next moment he was lying face down in a pool of his own blood, the bodyguard who'd been hired to protect him holding a smoking gun. That kind of thing happened all the time around here. It was impossible not to think about it.

Everywhere I looked, I saw guns. Guys in the street walked around in a way that let you know they were always there, ready to be drawn at any second and fired if you made the wrong move. I was drinking a lot back then. I got in fights at bars and slept at night without dreaming. Every day was like a waking nightmare.

I still made runs. By then it was routine, like punching a clock. I'd go to wherever the car was, get in, and drive it over the border. Then I'd wait in some diner while it all got unloaded and get back in when the car came back. Most of my payments came from Memo's wife, who seemed perfectly fine with the way her husband made a living.

My wife, on the other hand, was starting to ask questions. I began to slip up when I told her my fake stories. Soon, I knew, she'd ask the question I'd been dreading for months.

What the hell are you doing down there, John?

But I managed to throw her off the scent. Every time we talked, I'd obfuscate and steer the conversation in odd directions. I figured that eventually a moment would come when I'd break down and tell her everything. But I didn't have time to stop and plan for the future back then. I was just trying to get through the days without getting killed. I was just happy that I'd been able to scrape together enough money to pay for David's foot surgery, which I had delivered to the doctor myself.

I didn't like lying, though. Something about it grated on me. Compared to lying to my wife, dealing drugs was nothing. To deal with the guilt, I kept drinking hard. There were some mornings when I would wake up with an empty bottle of vodka by the bed, not remembering how I'd gotten there or what day it was. I partied all the time. My friends in the cartel loved it. We'd all hang around at night drinking and talking. I'd give them spiritual advice while girls danced on the table. I was never unfaithful, but I wasn't in my right mind.

I started getting used to the power that dealing with the cartel brought me. I liked that people called me *Papa John*. Sometimes I'd imagine that my life was a movie and I was the antihero. Around this time the show *Ozark* got big on Netflix. I watched it during the day while waiting to go on runs, imagining a future in which I built my own drug-smuggling empire based in Cabo San Lucas. As time went on, I started talking with David about it. He hated it. Every time I brought it up, he'd tell me I was going to get killed.

Thinking about those last days today, I cringe. I barely remember what it was like to be that person. My brain was foggy. I had no concept of the future. My son, whom I had tried so hard to protect from danger, was now in more trouble than he'd ever been in. No matter how many times I tried to help him out, he found himself back in a ditch surrounded by jackals. The kid was like a magnet for scumbags.

One of them was a member of the Hells Angels Motorcycle Club who'd fallen in with David in Cabo. For a few weeks the guy had stayed in my house, telling David he was just there to party. They'd done drugs and hung out late into the night, feeding scraps of their food to the mean dog the guy had brought with him. Then, brandishing a gun, the guy kicked David out of the house and told him to scram.

As soon as I learned on the phone that this had happened, I fumed. By then I'd begun to feel like I was a real member of the cartel—a guy who shouldn't be messed with. I made a few calls and requested a personal escort to go to the house and kick the guy out. Around this time, my best friend, Lance, called me and said that he and his wife had booked a cruise, which happened to be leaving from San Pedro in a few days. I figured it would be a good way for me to get down to Cabo, where I was going to have cartel escorts to help me kick the Hells Angel out of my house, without having to fly. Much to my shame, I asked Michelle if she wanted to come along, pitching the whole thing as a romantic getaway. She didn't want to go, but eventually I convinced her to come along.

In November 2017, we set sail.

The cruise was a nightmare.

The first time we hit land near Cabo, I drove out to the house with a couple of guys from the cartel. I found David and Arisbeth sleeping in an abandoned apartment, and we went straight to the house, where I confronted the Hells Angel, telling him he needed to vacate my house immediately. Because of the guys I'd brought along, he listened, and David and I spent the night at the house. The next morning, we drove to meet the cruise at the next stop, and I rejoined Michelle, who had figured out that something was going on.

Some nights, it worked. I drank too much, but no one noticed. On a cruise, overindulging in alcohol wasn't exactly uncommon. But Michelle could tell there was more to my trouble than the usual demons. During meals, she'd go silent and stare off at the horizon. I'd ask what was wrong, and she'd say nothing. Looking back, I can see she had a horrible feeling about what I was doing—she wasn't stupid, after all—but wouldn't say anything to me for fear of finding out too much.

We got through the cruise by not speaking much. We met people from all over the world, and I chatted with them at length about their lives. The feeling reminded me of speaking to parishioners at Living Hope, listening to their problems and giving them off-the-cuff advice. When it came to other people, I always seemed to know exactly what they should do. When it came to my own life, not so much.

On one of our last nights on the cruise, Michelle confronted me about everything.

"I know you're lying to me," she said. "And I can't take it anymore. Whatever is going on in Mexico with you, it needs to stop. I can't take the lies, John. I can't."

We sat in silence for a long time, staring at the skyline, watching the coastline of Cabo San Lucas come slowly back into view.

I decided I was done.

"The car's loaded," Memo said. "You can't just *not* do it."

I'd called him as soon as the boat docked, trying to stay out of earshot of Michelle. He'd known right away I was going to give him trouble.

"I don't know what to tell you, man. I'm done."

"No, you're not."

I felt another flare of anger in my gut. After all the history I'd had with this guy, I was finally beginning to see that he saw me as an idiot. To him, I was nothing more than a disposable, gullible old man who drove his product across the border. He didn't care whether I lived or died. If I crossed him, he'd have no problem killing me. I'd known that for years, of course; but there's a difference between knowing something and *knowing* it.

"I can't do it."

He sighed, finally realizing I was serious.

"What the fuck?" he said.

"I just can't do it."

A few seconds of silence passed between us.

"Just do one more," he said. "I need you to take this one more load across, we'll pay you, and then you can be done. I swear. This can be your last time."

I looked over at Michelle, who was waiting for me at the edge of the water. I'd told her I was making a business call, and she'd had enough sense to walk away while I did it. She looked beautiful standing in the fading sunlight. I wanted nothing more than to get on a plane and fly back home with her, even if it meant poverty and long hours struggling as a cashier at a grocery store. In my mind, I told Memo to fuck off, enjoying the way the words felt coming out of my mouth.

But I didn't say them.

"Fine," I said. "One more time. Then I'm out."

I put the phone back in my pocket and walked over to Michelle. She looked at me like she was seeing me for the last time.

A few hours later we were in front of Memo's house in the hills of Tijuana. Unlike the place where I lived, it was quiet. Giant houses sat far back from the street. Most of the windows were dark. Michelle pulled our car over to the side of the road and parked a few feet from Memo's driveway.

When she turned to look at me, there were tears in her eyes.

"You don't have to do this," she said.

I didn't know what to say.

For the past few years I'd been aware on some level that I didn't *have* to do anything I was doing. I could have stopped anytime. No one was holding a gun to my head and forcing me to stay in Cabo San Lucas, although they were using my son as a pawn. But something about staying there had made me feel important again. People needed me there. They *liked* me there. In the absence of the church that I had worked so hard to build, being needed had felt good—even if I was needed by people who couldn't have cared less about whether I lived or died.

I was glad to be getting out.

Michelle said it again, louder this time.

"You don't have to do this."

I nodded, saying nothing for once.

"I know," I said. "But it's one more time. Then it's a new life for us. I promise. I'll be all done down here."

I got out of the car to walk down the street.

She sped ahead of me and drove out of the neighborhood. Out of Tijuana, then out of Mexico.

I stepped into Memo's house and got ready to drive.

Chapter 25

The last run began like all the others.

Memo and I left his house and drove to a parking lot, where my gray Volkswagen was parked. Things were awkward between us, but he didn't mention anything about the phone call from last night. He just slid into a parking spot, put his car in Park, and looked out the window.

"You ready?" he said.

I told him I was.

"Same as always. Slide into the lane. Look for the text. We'll tell you where to go."

I got behind the wheel and pulled the visor down to block out the sun. I didn't bother to check the bottom to make sure the bags were all secured. I'd done so many runs at this point that the thought of getting caught barely occurred to me anymore. I figured the cartel had paid off enough border guards to make it almost impossible. Driving down the highway, I had a feeling that I was being pulled on a string toward the checkpoint, operating on autopilot, just going where I was supposed to be going. Free will seemed to have very little to do with it.

A few minutes later I was on my knees at the border checkpoint, lacing my fingers behind my head and trying to ignore the screaming pain in my knees. The border guards barked orders and pointed guns in my face. I closed my eyes and prayed. Looking back,

I can see that there was something inevitable about the moment. A guy on the verge of going straight finally gets caught, and no one believes him because he's strung out on booze. For a moment I wondered whether I was still asleep in my bed on the cruise ship, having the familiar nightmare of getting caught during one of my runs.

But the cold touch of the handcuffs on my wrists was very real. So was the hand that gripped me by the shoulder and shoved me away from the car toward a small building by the checkpoint. I stumbled inside to the sound of blaring car horns and shouted commands from the other guards, thinking about my wife and my children and all the ways I'd failed them again. My knees ached.

I prayed, looking for some answer from God about what to do.

Nothing came.

Two guards chained me to a metal bench in a cell. A few other guys sat around me, all looking similarly shocked and dismayed that they'd been caught.

I wondered whether any of us worked for the same people. It wasn't outside the realm of possibility. Over the years, I'd seen Memo take hundreds of phone calls, switching between English and Spanish. For all I knew, he had dozens of guys just like me running drugs for him, all equally disposable.

Then it hit me.

Now that I was caught, Memo was going to have to check up on my family, Michelle especially. I could imagine him walking up to her house in Yuma, knocking on the front door, and refusing to leave until she let him inside. I could see him sitting down and putting his gun on the table, just like Chucho had done to me during our first meeting, and telling her everything.

I looked around at the other guys in the cell with me. A few looked high on hard drugs. They smelled bad. Two of them talked to each other, telling stories about friends they had in common. I shook my head. As strange as it might sound, I still viewed these guys as scumbag drug runners. In my mind, they were trafficking poison into the United States, some of which would probably end up in my hometown of Vancouver. I thought about all the nights I'd wanted to find the guy selling my son heroin and beat him to death.

I wondered if these guys had any shame about what they were doing. Didn't they know that the shit they were trafficking killed people? Didn't they know it made people's teeth fall out and slowly drained the life from their bodies until there was nothing left? I felt like spitting at them.

Then something else hit me, and the room began to spin.

I'd never seen the underside of my car. Not even once. I'd never pulled off the door panels and inspected the product these guys were stuffing in. For all I knew, there *could* have been heroin in there the whole time. There could have been meth or guns or a dead body. I would have had no idea. It's not like I could tell any difference in the weight.

I looked around, trying to get some indication of what was going on. Right now, I knew, a group of guards was searching my car. What they found would determine what happened to me next. If it was just weed, I'd probably get a month in prison for every pound. That's what the cartel guys had always told me.

But again, I hadn't looked it up.

I had no idea what was going on.

I leaned my head back on the concrete wall and closed my eyes, trying to pray again. If there was ever a time for me to get a message from God the way I used to when I was a pastor, it would have been then. I had never felt so powerless and alone. The cartel had good reason to hurt members of my family—my daughters, my wife, my son—and for once, there was nothing I could do to protect them.

Again, nothing came.

All morning, guards came in and out of the holding area to speak with the detainees. Sometimes they were nice, offering sandwiches and sodas, leading them out for quick interviews in the small conference rooms along the hallway. A few of the guys they led into these rooms got to go other places.

I knew what that meant.

In a situation like this, you were useless to the authorities. What they really wanted was information on the people you were working for. If you agreed to give it to them, they might shave a few years off your sentence. They might let you go altogether, making you promise never to run drugs again.

I knew a lot of guys. *This* time, if the FBI came around and asked about what I knew about the operations of the Sinaloa Cartel, I could have led them to some pretty high-profile people. I could have given them addresses of drop sites, phone numbers, and lists of names a mile long. I could have bought my freedom in five minutes.

But that would mark me and my family for death.

Michelle would have been lying on the floor of her kitchen with a bullet hole in her head before I could even get my release papers signed. David would have gone down shortly thereafter, along with my daughters and their families. When it came to retaliation against rats, there was nothing the cartel wouldn't do. They'd drive up to Manhattan and shoot someone in the middle of Broadway if it meant sending a message to anyone even *thinking* about informing on them to the federal government.

I decided I was going to stay quiet.

When two agents came and unlocked my chains, I barely looked at them. When they led me into a room and began asking me questions, I stayed quiet.

One of them told me what was going on.

"Listen, Mr. Bishop," he said, putting his pen down on the table and sighing. "Right now, we've got guys going through your car, and all they've found is marijuana. If that's all they end up finding, then good. You'll go to prison, but not for long. But if we find anything else, which we usually do in cases like this? You're going away for a long time. Unless you work with us."

I shook my head and said nothing.

The two agents tried a few other angles of approach. I found myself wanting to tell them everything, desperately trying to stop myself from speaking. My head was pounding from a lack of alcohol and nerves. The buzz of the fluorescent light above my head was driving me nuts. I felt sweaty and tired and stupid and lost.

In the end, I managed to keep my mouth shut.

The agents led me out of the room and back to my cell. On the way, I stuck a hand in the pocket of my shorts and felt something small and hard. They'd taken my phone and my wallet as soon as I came inside, but not whatever this was.

Back on the metal bench, once I was sure no agents were looking, I took the object out and looked at it. The clear color and rough texture gave it away.

Meth.

Over the past few months, I'd dabbled in hard drugs. So had the people around me. I wasn't surprised that there was a little left over, although I was surprised that the border patrol agents hadn't caught it. Given what I'd just been told about the consequences of finding anything other than weed on my person, I decided there was only one way out of the situation.

I checked one more time to make sure no agents were watching, popped the meth in my mouth like a potato chip, and swallowed.

The buzz hit me immediately. The bars in front of my face went a little fuzzy, and my heart began racing. I wondered how David had managed to take hits of this so regularly and still form sentences. Luckily, no one else in the cell had seen me swallow it, so I didn't have to worry about sharing. I doubled over and tapped my foot like crazy, seeing the events of the past few years play out in a sped-up, demented loop.

I saw Chucho piling up cocaine on the table in front of me, then the crowd at Living Hope standing up to pray. I saw David cooking up heroin in a motel room and Memo pointing toward the loaded-up Volkswagen he'd bought for me. Michelle and my daughters and Neal Curtiss. Guns. Knives. The closed casket they'd buried Chucho in out in the desert, and the hundreds of tiny white crosses that stuck out of the sand. The whole thing was like a nightmare I couldn't wake up from.

I came out of my meth-induced haze long enough to see two agents unlocking my cuffs and leading me down a dark hallway toward another cell.

This must be where they put the people who don't make deals, I thought.

The visions continued as I walked into my new cell—which was empty—and sat down on another cold metal bench. The agents didn't bother to bolt me in this time. They just closed the door and left me to sit there.

I couldn't stop thinking.

Finally, as the meth wore off, I found myself thinking about the last sermons I'd delivered at Living Hope—the ones about Elijah and how far he ran because he was scared of what the Lord had in store for him. I always knew that eventually I would reach my personal end of the road. There were nights when I thought that would be a bullet in the head. Sometimes I thought it would be a nice quiet life with Michelle.

Sitting in the dim cell alone, where I ended up staying for just over twenty hours, I realized exactly what the end of the road for me was.

Prison.

Part 4

65782-298

Chapter 26

By about eleven o'clock the next night, I was twenty miles away in San Diego, standing in front of four prison guards in nothing but my underwear.

I didn't know the guards' names, but they knew mine. For the past five minutes or so, one of them had used it at the end of every instruction he'd given me.

Arms up, Bishop.

I'm going to search you now, Bishop.

Remove your clothes, Bishop.

Now, I knew, there was only one step left. But knowing what was coming didn't make it any less mortifying.

"Alright," said the guard. "Pull down your underwear and bend over at the waist, Bishop. Then grab your butt cheeks, spread them, and cough."

I closed my eyes and complied.

After two or three heavy coughs—apparently, my first one wasn't quite forceful enough to push out any drugs that might have been stuffed up my butt—I was allowed to stand up.

The guard, who seemed pretty used to this process, handed me a pile of clothes to put on. From now on, everything I wore would be prison-issued. I'd get two uniform shirts, two pairs of pants, two undershirts, and one pair of white slip-on shoes. They even supplied two pairs of white boxers, one of which I pulled on quickly as the guard asked me some questions.

"Any gang affiliations?" he asked.

I said no.

"Any rivalries?"

No.

"Any tattoos?"

Seriously, buddy? I thought. *If there's anyone who should know the answer to that one, it's you. You just saw parts of my body that no one has seen since I was a baby.*

But I didn't say that.

Instead, I answered calmly, using mostly one-word answers. I figured that eventually I might get on good enough terms with the guards to joke around a little. Especially this guy, who seemed not to hate my guts as much as his three friends. But for now, my main job was to keep my head down and act like a model prisoner.

After a few more questions, the guard lowered his clipboard and handed me a stack of papers. On top, there was an eight-digit number.

"*That*," said the guard, pointing at the papers with his pen, "is your number. In here, it's your identity. You'll use it to schedule medical appointments, interact with the staff, and purchase items at the commissary once a week. Memorize that number, and do *not* forget it."

Looking down, I tried to commit the eight digits to memory: 65782–298. But it wasn't going very well. My hands were shaking, and my head was pounding. The past thirty hours or so hadn't exactly been great for my cognitive abilities. Luckily, I'd have plenty of time with this little slip of paper to get it right.

When I looked up, the guard was standing in front of me with a thin, hard mattress that had been rolled up like a yoga mat. In prison, this is called a bedroll. He held it out and said it was time to get to my cell, which would be on the sixth floor of the prison.

Suddenly, I panicked. Everything was happening too fast.

For some reason, it hit me then, seeing the mattress I would be sleeping on for the first time, that I was *really* in prison and that I couldn't leave.

Then something else hit me.

"Before we go," I said to the guard, "I just—I'm not sure who to talk to about this, but . . ."

He said nothing.

"Well, I've been drinking pretty heavily lately. And, like, for the past few years. The last time I went this long without a drink was . . . I don't even remember when. I think I'm going to have some serious problems with—"

"Withdrawal?"

"Yes, sir. Shakes, stomach cramps. All that."

To demonstrate, I held one wobbly hand out in front of me, palm down.

The guard sighed. Apparently, I wasn't the first washed-up criminal to come through this tiny concrete room and complain about alcohol withdrawal.

Before I could say anything else about my symptoms, one of the guards launched into a speech. From the sound of it, I assumed it was one he'd probably given a few dozen times already that week.

"We can get you to a hospital," he said. "We'd be more than happy to do that. But once you get there, the nurse is going to handcuff you to the hospital bed and secure your legs too. You'll get the drugs you're looking for, but you'll have to stay for seven days, until they clear you."

I took a moment before responding.

Obviously, there was one right answer, which is the one I gave.

"I'll just go cold turkey here. No problem."

The guard nodded, handed me a bedroll, and led me into a

waiting room. I sat there for the next hour or so, then walked into a third room, where I answered some more questions for a woman behind a desk. At some point, she asked if I wanted to be placed in protective custody because of my age.

I was fifty-four and probably looked at least ten years older than that, but for some reason, I declined the offer. In the days that followed, I would come to regret that decision, chalking it up to withdrawal-induced delirium or just plain old stupidity.

After that meeting was done, one of the guards who'd conducted my cavity search came back into the room and told me to follow him. I was going to a cell on the sixth floor, he said, and I'd have two cellmates. Given that it was after midnight, he wanted me to walk into the cell, go to sleep, and stay quiet.

I said I would. In prison, as I would learn over the next few years, you'll often get orders like this. In the beginning, they make you feel like a child. Your first instinct is to lash out and tell the guy to get lost.

But you get used to it.

As we walked toward the cell, me with my bedroll and the guard with his clipboard, he explained a few more things about the way prison life worked. But I wasn't listening. All I could do was look around at the dark prison, staring into the cells and marveling at how quiet it was. For some reason, movies and television had led me to believe that prisoners howl like wild hyenas all through the night, shouting nonsensical phrases and threats until sunrise.

But there was nothing.

Somehow, that was worse than screaming.

After about five minutes, we arrived at my cell. The guard pressed a button and the door opened. Before I even stepped inside, I could hear one of my cellmates snoring. It sounded like someone was starting up the world's largest lawn mower.

I walked inside and began climbing up onto my bunk. Even in broad daylight, this would have been difficult. Here in the dark, it was nearly impossible. As I struggled with my bedroll, trying like hell not to disturb the two guys in the room—who, for all I knew, could have been murderous thugs dreaming sweet dreams about killing people—the guard said goodnight and closed the door.

As he left, I noticed that he wasn't using my name anymore.

Chapter 27

I didn't sleep much. The pain from detoxing made it hard to relax. In the morning I rolled over on my bunk and faced the cell's lone window. Through it I could see a massive white cruise ship that had docked in the harbor nearby. I shifted a little in the bunk and caught a glimpse of the name, which was barely visible in the low sunlight. Only then did I realize it was the same cruise ship I'd just been on with my wife—the one I'd stood in front of when I told Memo I would drive one more time.

Just a few days earlier I had been on that cruise ship drinking wine, eating good food, and making friends with the other tourists. I wanted to go back. I wanted to tell that guy to throw his phone into the ocean and drive home with Michelle. We could have figured it out.

But it was too late.

As I woke up slowly, I heard my two cellmates get up and begin talking to each other in Spanish. I crawled out of my bunk slowly, once again regretting that I had never bothered to learn the language.

We tried to talk for a while. But the language barrier made it almost impossible. Still, I was happy to find that they were nice guys. I got the sense that in here, that wasn't the norm. Over the next few hours, we did manage to negotiate a deal that would allow me to take the bottom bunk. I'd arrange to get them a few dollars a week in commissary, and they'd shift bunks to keep me from having to climb up to the top bunk again.

At some point that afternoon, I cried.

Then I went to a meeting with a woman who asked me a bunch of questions about my state of mind.

Then I cried again.

For the next seven days, I stuck to that schedule. I'd go to meetings with court-appointed lawyers, then come back and cry. I'd shower, shave with a plastic razor, then come back and cry. My wife was alone, probably getting threatened by Memo. I had no idea where David was. My daughters were about to get a brand-new reason to be ashamed of me. And here I was, sitting in prison, unable to get in touch with anyone, not even knowing how many years I was facing.

The first meeting with my lawyers was dismal and uninspiring. Both attorneys seemed interested only in reaching a deal with the US attorney. They let me know that because of the amount of marijuana that had been found in my car (about three hundred pounds), the sentencing guidelines said I should get somewhere between five and forty years. It was possible that I'd spend the rest of my life in prison.

To my surprise, I managed not to cry when they told me that. I just looked down, detached, and shook my head. I was shocked. I'd been assured by lying cartel members that there would never be more than a hundred pounds in the car.

I headed back to my cell and cried.

To get to the courtroom in San Diego, I took an elevator down to the prison basement and walked through a tunnel under the road. My legs and ankles were bound with chains. Beside me, a United States Marshal walked slowly, not saying much.

It wasn't until we were in the elevator on the way back up to the prison, after I had listened quietly to my charges on the advice of my lawyers, that he looked over at me and spoke.

"You know, I looked you up while you were in there," he said. "All the church stuff. The books. The sermons. What *happened* to you?"

I didn't know what to say.

Before I could think of an answer, the elevator let out a *ding*. The doors opened, and we walked back out into the prison. It began to sink in that after this initial week of appointments was over, there'd be nothing left for me to do but sit and wait for someone to post bond. At that first court hearing, I'd learned that someone would need to hand over $2,000 to bail me out of prison so I could prepare for trial.

I'd already tried calling Michelle. Each time, her phone had gone straight to voicemail. At MCC San Diego, prisoners were allowed to make one fifteen-minute phone call a day. Over the course of my first seven days, I made seven phone calls, all to Michelle. Finally, after a week of trying to reach her, I called friends whose numbers I knew by heart.

Every one of them told me they couldn't help.

A few people gave no reason. One of my relatives said he was afraid I'd flee the country if I got out on bail. The only exception was Lance, who'd been on the cruise with me and Michelle. I'd considered Lance a close friend for years. He and his wife, Carolyn, had always been fun to hang out with. But I never thought he'd support me in the way he did. He certainly didn't have to, after all I'd done to Living Hope and its parishioners. But he said he'd see what he could do about posting bond and getting me out of prison. He also said he'd put a few dollars on my commissary account, which would allow me to pay for things like non-prison food and toiletries.

A few days later, on "commissary day," which was only once a week and very much looked forward to, I stood in line in front of the counter with all the other prisoners, waiting my turn to make purchases. This took about an hour, given how many prisoners there were. By the time I got to the front of the line, my knees ached. I'd almost forgotten what I wanted in the first place. I knew I was screwed as soon as I stepped up to the counter.

"Hey, I'm new here, and I think I need—"

"Number," said the woman behind the glass.

Oh no.

The words of that first guard came back to me.

"Don't forget your number" was the one piece of advice I'd gotten since I showed up here, and I'd managed to forget it.

I was asked to step aside for the prisoners who *actually* had their shit together, and the next guy stepped up. As I walked away from the line, guys shouted "Prez" and "Donald Trump" at me. I didn't know what they were talking about until I caught my reflection in a piece of metal along the wall. Then I remembered the barbershop.

A few weeks earlier I had stumbled into an empty barbershop in Tijuana and asked for a haircut. The woman there, who'd been sweeping when I walked in, agreed, though she didn't speak much English. She put me in a chair facing away from the mirror and got to work, never letting me see her progress. Then, after about thirty minutes, she turned me around and showed me what she'd done to me. The hair was coiffed and swooped up in a strawberry-blond wave, making me look like the spitting image of the forty-fifth president of the United States. When I went back the next morning and asked for some adjustments, the salon owner asked who'd cut my hair. When I described the woman who'd given me the Donald Trump look, the owner said, "Oh, her? That's my sister! She doesn't cut hair. Just sweeps." And so here I was, locked in a building with hundreds of Mexican guys looking like I was dressed up as Donald J. Trump—who, as it turned out, was even less popular with the Mexican people than you might imagine at the time.

As the taunts kept coming, I ran back to my cell to try to find the paperwork I'd been given upon my arrival. But it was no use. Commissary hours were over by the time I found it. Once again, I probably cried. It's hard to remember. I cried so much that first week that I got physically tired from it. Between the constant sobbing and the alcohol withdrawal, I did very little other than shake and feel sorry for myself.

The lowest point, though, came about two weeks into my detention, during a meeting with my lawyers.

"We got these this morning," said one of them.

I looked at the table, where he'd placed an envelope addressed to me. I opened it, took out the papers, and scanned the top page.

I saw Michelle's name immediately.

"This is common," said the lawyer, trying to make me feel better about the situation.

I flipped through the packet, seeing the words *legal* and *separation* a few times. That was all I needed to throw the papers back down on the table and hang my head. Over the past few days, I'd heard that divorce was all but inevitable for guys in prison. Eventually wives and girlfriends stopped waiting for you.

I don't know why I thought Michelle, who'd been through unbearable pain because of me already, would be any different. And who would blame her?

For the rest of the meeting, the lawyers' words sounded like mumbling. I couldn't listen to them. All I could do was think about the way Michelle had looked at me in the car in front of Memo's house, practically begging me to drive away with her. I realized, sitting here, how easy it would have been to just run away. To the cartel, I was worth nothing. They probably wouldn't have even looked for me. Instead of sitting on a hard metal chair with two bargain-brand public defenders (which many of the inmates called "public pretenders"), I could have been asleep next to my wife, preparing to go to a job selling cars or cleaning floors.

I could have worked my way back to being a pastor again.

When the meeting was over, I wandered out into the wide-open space where prisoners gathered for an hour a day, holding my separation papers in one hand like the corpse of a dead animal. One guy gave me a look like he knew exactly what had just happened to me. Walking around, I wondered what to do. I didn't know anyone. All around me, prisoners who'd been entrusted with small jobs around the prison handed out hot water for tea, coffee, and ramen noodles. We called these prisoners "trustees." Guys munched on candy bars and lifted weights in the corner.

I felt lost. I remembered trying to find one single thing I could control. I wanted a simple task that I could complete other than wiping tears from my face. It didn't matter how inane or stupid it was.

So I got a haircut.

The prison barber at MCC San Diego was a six-foot-three transgender woman named Miss Ricky. I sat in her chair with my separation papers under my butt, noticing for the first time how long and shaggy I'd allowed my hair to get over the past few months. Once, at the height of Living Hope's success, a newspaper reporter had described me as looking just like Sammy Hagar.

Now I looked like someone had taken Sammy Hagar's fat, homeless cousin and dragged him behind a truck for a few hours.

But Miss Ricky didn't care.

As she began running a comb through my hair, she asked how I was doing, sensing I was new before I even said anything.

I answered by bawling my eyes out.

A *lot*.

At that moment she could have told me a few things. The story of her own life, for instance. Years ago, before she got locked up, Miss Ricky had been a Golden Glove boxer. At her first prison in San Quentin, she'd begun medically transitioning from a man to a woman, which had earned her nothing but contempt from the inmates. Two guys had tried to beat her to death in a cell, which was how she'd ended up here for a psychological evaluation, among other things. But she didn't tell me any of that. I learned it later from a few guys in my pod.

Instead, she told me to stop crying.

And I did.

"You can't be doing that in here," she said. "This isn't about you."

I asked what she meant.

"Your wife is out there, on the outside. But really, she's locked up with you. She worries about you. So does everyone who loves you. *They're* the ones you should be crying for. Not yourself. What you need to focus on for the next couple years, or however long it takes, is doing your time. Don't let your time do you."

There was more like that. For the rest of the haircut, Miss Ricky talked, and I listened. It was a nice change of pace, being the person *getting* the life advice rather than giving it.

And it worked.

That morning sitting in the barber's chair was the last time I cried in prison.

Every time I went to court, there was a guy from the cartel sitting in the back. He never announced himself, but I knew who he was.

Sitting in front of the judge, listening to the rules and procedures, I'd always be able to feel that guy's presence.

Talk, he seemed to say, *and we'll kill your family.*

All of them.

After a little more than a month in prison, a guard approached my cell and let me know that I'd made bail.

"Roll it up, Bishop," he said, referring to the hard bedroll I'd been sleeping on for the past thirty days.

I popped up on my aching knees and said goodbye to my cellmates. Then I ran up to the guard and wrapped him in a big bear hug, giggling like a little schoolgirl. He pushed me away and backed up like I'd just kissed him on the mouth.

"Get your shit," he said. "And don't ever hug me again."

I walked out into the bright sunshine for the first time in what felt like years, breathing in the warm air. Just before I left, I had given away all my possessions, as was customary for prisoners who were about to go free. I hadn't realized how bad prison smelled until I walked out to this parking lot. Over the past few days I'd been talking to people about my situation. Most of them believed that once I got out on pre-trial bond, I probably wouldn't have to go back to prison. Given my age and the fact that I wasn't a flight risk, the court would probably be fine with allowing me to check in with a probation officer every week rather than serving a sentence, as long as I found a job and kept my head down.

That sounded good to me.

I was about to get a cab when I looked across the street and saw a familiar car.

It was Michelle's.

Standing beside it, still looking scared to death, was my wife of thirty-five years.

Standing there in the parking lot, I cried.

But the reunion was bittersweet. On the long drive back to

Yuma, Arizona, Michelle told me everything that had happened to her over the past month. She'd only learned that I'd been arrested when Memo pulled up to her in a car and threatened her and the kids. He said he knew the addresses of our daughters, our grandchildren, and Michelle's parents, any of whom the cartel would kill if I decided to talk.

And she had dealt with it all alone, unable to tell anyone what we were going through for fear that it would mean the death of the people she loved most in the world. She'd legally separated from me on the advice of her lawyer, knowing that it was better not to be married to a person going through my situation. But she wasn't going to leave me, provided I got my act together.

Seeing her again, even in a prison parking lot, made me happier than I'd ever been in my life.

For the next seven months Michelle and I lived in a single-wide trailer in Yuma that we'd purchased after we sold the house in Vancouver. It was about the size of the first home we'd ever lived in together, barely big enough for us both to stand in at the same time. But she decorated it in such a way that I always felt warm and happy walking in the door.

David flew out shortly after I got released, and we decided to go into business together. I was surprised by how well he looked. After my arrest, he said, he'd been spooked into turning over a new leaf. It had been weeks since he'd used drugs.

If getting arrested was what it took, I thought, *then fine. As long as you're safe.*

We could have picked any industry. But we settled on a diesel engine repair business with the help of my good friend Namon Martin, working right from the house. If it wasn't for Namon, I don't know what David and I would have done. Every week,

I would check in with a parole officer, who made me pee in a cup while he watched and answer a few questions. Other than the first meeting, when I got too nervous to urinate in front of him, things were going well. I met with my lawyer, a public defender, and learned that I would, in all likelihood, be able to avoid going back to prison.

Friends wrote letters attesting to my character. At the end of my seven months in Yuma, I had more than 150 of them, all from people whose lives I had touched over the years. Just hearing the number was enough to make me emotional. Reading through them, holding back tears, I began to get a sense of myself as a good person. I felt a sense of hope rising inside me that the judge would see that, too, and allow me to serve the rest of my time out here with my wife and my children.

As we got closer to the date of the hearing that would decide my fate, that hope intensified.

I felt like God was back on my side, guiding every step that I took.

Everything was going to be okay.

Chapter 28

Tap, tap.

Tap, tap, tap, tap-tap-tap.

My lawyer tapped his pen on a blank yellow legal pad in front of him. The judge made his way slowly to the bench as I sat sweating at the defense table.

I checked behind me for the sicario. He was there, right in the back of the room, where I knew he would be.

Worst-case scenario, I knew, I would get six more months. Maybe a year. But now that I knew Michelle had no intention of divorcing me for real, and that David would be set up with our business, I could do a year without much of a problem.

Tap, tap, tap.

The sound was all I could hear. I asked the lawyer to stop, and he nodded.

We stood up as the judge called the session to order. Then we sat back down, and the tapping started again.

That morning I had taken one last look around my living room in Yuma. Although I'd been told that I would probably be back that afternoon, I had a feeling that I wouldn't see it again for a long time. Somewhere in the back of my mind, the voice of God told me that I still had to come to terms with a few things.

I tried to push that voice down and hope for the best as the judge began his hearing.

The prosecutor got up and laid into me, telling the judge I was a drug kingpin, a flight risk, and other things you really don't want to have said about you in a court of law. Listening to her, even my best friend in the world would have thought I was a cold-blooded monster who lived to cause misery to other people. I got the sense that all 150 letters people had written about me weren't going to matter.

Not if the judge believed this woman's story.

Which, I realized at the time, wasn't totally wrong. I *had* hurt people, even if I'd done so inadvertently. I had thought about starting my own smuggling operation. Worst of all, as far as the government was concerned, was my refusal to give up information on the people I was working with—or to talk about anything I had done. Over the past few months, I'd heard from my lawyer that if I said Michelle had known about what I was doing, I might get out of prison.

That was out of the question. I had deceived my wife, and I wasn't going to pretend she'd had something to do with my crimes just to make a court happy. If I had to go to prison for the rest of my life because of that, I was willing to do it.

The prosecutor finished and produced a three-ring binder filled with about three hundred pages' worth of bad stuff about me. In it, there were vivid descriptions of a criminal conspiracy I had supposedly run as well as messages from my phone—many of them sent while I was drunk—that made me sound like a raving psycho. With that evidence, any judge would have sent me right back to prison for a year.

But not this one.

At the close of the hearing, as reporters from the local newspaper scribbled furiously on their notepads in the back, the judge said a few words about what a low-life, unrepentant scumbag I was.

Tap, tap.

". . . standards for waiving the mandatory minimum sentencing have not been met . . ."

Tap, tap, tap, tap.

". . . John Lee Bishop, ordered to be remanded to custody."

The tapping stopped.

I turned to my lawyer and repeated the word *remanded*, which was brand-new to me.

His face, a blank stare, told me what it meant.

"Is this really happening?"

"Yes," he said. "It's really happening."

And that was it.

I stood up, and a US Marshal put cuffs on my wrists. I turned to Michelle, who had tears in her eyes. Tears streamed down my face too. I looked long enough to see David hug Michelle before a Marshal told me in a stern voice to keep my eyes forward.

"Don't look at anyone in the courtroom," he said.

Then he took my arm, led me through a door, and we walked together down a long, empty hallway.

After a few steps he began to speak freely.

"Man," he said. "I looked you up . . ."

Just like the last guy, I thought.

". . . the church, the books. What happened to you?"

I still didn't have a good answer.

A few nights later I lay on the floor of a holding cell at GEO Western Region Detention Facility in downtown San Diego, shaking with what I'd later learn was a bad case of pneumonia. As I moved in and out of my fever dreams, I had vivid hallucinations about the hearing that had just occurred. In my mind I was a free man, sleeping in my bed back in Yuma, and the past few days were only a nightmare.

But they weren't.

I'd been fingerprinted again. I'd been handed prison-issue

clothes and put right back in a cell. Only this one was smaller, and I had to share it with ten illegal immigrants on the verge of being deported. There were no beds, so we all slept on the floor, which I was now curled up on with a rough blanket over my body, just a few feet from the toilet.

I smelled urine and body odor. I missed my wife. Ahead of me was *five years* of prison. I had no idea what it was going to feel like, given that my thirty days in prison had been almost unbearable. One weekend had almost shut my body down. I didn't know how I would make it through another hour, let alone a few more days.

One Saturday, before I was set to be driven to a real prison, my lawyer visited. He told me I had one more shot to implicate others in my crimes.

"The judge might be willing to rethink the sentence at our next hearing if you give up some information," he said.

"Would you rat on guys who could hurt your family?" I asked him.

The conversation didn't end on a positive note.

Settling back into being incarcerated was like riding a bike.

Without the seat.

Every step I took was agony. Every time someone gave me an order—which, in prison, happens every few seconds—I felt a little piece of me die inside. Before long, the jumpsuit and the slip-on shoes were familiar again. The feel of the fluorescent lights on my skin felt normal. I was operating on autopilot, just trying to get through the day.

One afternoon a man in a suit came up and spoke to me through the bars of my cell. I noticed him right away, as we didn't tend to see many guys in suits in prison. He asked me if I was John Bishop.

I told him I was.

"I *knew* it!" he said. "I used to show your messages all the time to my guys. They were so inspiring. Guys could really understand what you were talking about, and . . ."

Please, I thought, *don't say, "What happened to you?"*

He didn't. Instead, he told me he was the prison chaplain and that he still had a bunch of videos I'd made as the pastor of Living Hope on VHS. I thought of all the tapes that had been destroyed when I got fired, happy that they still existed somewhere, even if that place was a prison chaplain's office.

For the next few minutes, the chaplain told me what my messages had meant to prisoners he'd known over the years. The guys in the holding cell with me started listening. When the chaplain left, they asked about the Bible and how to start reading it. I tried to give them good advice.

The next day, a guy who looked meaner than everyone else on the block put together approached me in the open space outside our cells. His name was Adam, and he was waiting to be released back to Mexico.

Adam went down a list of his sins, counting them off on his fingers. He'd killed many people. He'd lied and cheated on his wife and done some other things that even he couldn't bring himself to say out loud. He asked me, a pastor, whether I could forgive him. I told him I didn't need to forgive him. And that was the beginning of a relationship that lasted for the next three weeks, until I got transferred to another prison.

During that time I learned that Adam was the "shot caller" on our block. That meant he'd worked his way to the top of the hierarchy for a certain gang, usually through violence. Nothing could happen in the prison—not sanctioned fights, drug deals, or even conversations—unless he said it was okay. He "had the keys," to use a little more prison lingo.

Sometime in October a guard came by my cell and told me to "roll it up" again. But I didn't jump up and hug this guy. I didn't even smile. This time I wasn't going home. I was going to federal holding at Santa Ana Prison, one of the most violent places in the country. During my time at GEO, I'd heard stories about Santa Ana. Prisoners there all belonged to violent gangs. The guards didn't let you pool your money and order pizza the way they did here in the cushy, minimum-security environment of GEO.

I walked down the hallway, bedroll in hand, trying to find Adam so I could say goodbye. But I never found him.

A few minutes later I was chained to a hard seat in a van, driving west.

Alone.

Chapter 29

About forty guys stood in the lobby of the prison in Santa Ana, all waiting to be processed. The room smelled like death. All I could see were tattooed arms and scars. All I could hear were Spanish curses, coughing, and the faraway sound of someone sobbing.

Been there, brother, I thought.

After a few minutes the guards began forming the crowd into a single-file line. At the front, a woman stood behind a camera, preparing to photograph each prisoner one by one. A few other guys still milled around in the corner. No one told me what to do.

So I got in line.

As the guys up ahead took their turns, I got the rhythm of whatever this was. You got to the front of the line, took your shirt off, and posed for the camera. The woman told you to turn around, you turned around, and then you were done. It seemed easy enough.

Again, I was the odd man out in this room. Everyone else was skinny and Mexican. I was fat and paler than paper, my suntan having faded months ago. When I stepped to the front of the line, the woman took her face away from the camera and stared at me, eyebrow cocked. I lifted my shirt over my head, revealing my giant stomach and man boobs. Audible giggles broke out behind me.

"What the hell are you doing?" said the photographer.

I stood there, shirt in one hand, not quite knowing how to answer. "I thought . . ."

"Do you have any tattoos, Bishop?"

"Well, one . . ."

I held out my right hand, where I have a small tattoo between my first and second fingers.

She shook her head and sighed.

"Get out of the line please. And put your shirt back on. For *all* of us."

I went and sat against the wall, happy I'd given everyone something to laugh about for a few minutes.

Then we went inside.

And everyone stopped laughing.

Everywhere I looked, there were angry dudes. At the time, Santa Ana was (and probably still is) a place where other prisons sent their most violent offenders. Shortly after my arrival, I sat down with a woman in a small office on the first floor of the prison to talk about placement. She asked if I wanted to be put in protective custody because of my age.

I said no.

To this day, I'm not sure why. It probably had something to do with my need to connect with people. Although I hated every second of being incarcerated, I still look back fondly on the people I met. And it wasn't like the threat of violence was going to sway me at all. I'd been dealing with violent people (myself included) all my life. Even as a middle-aged fat guy, I figured I would be able to take care of myself.

There was something deeper too. Somewhere in the back of my mind, I got the feeling that God wanted me out among the prisoners. That experience with the prison chaplain had reminded me what it felt like to change people's lives through God. Soon, I knew, I would be able to get back to doing that.

But I had to get my bearings first.

In November 2018, I was shackled and driven back to San Diego, where a judge officially sentenced me to five years in prison. Despite a letter that I'd written to the judge making my case—a letter he read in full to the room, which took about eleven minutes—there was nothing he could do.

The first days back in Santa Ana were rough.

For starters, I wasn't quite prepared for the extent to which race mattered in prison. The Mexicans hung with the Mexicans, the Blacks with the Blacks, and the whites with the whites. You broke ranks at your own peril.

Shortly after I arrived, I met the shot caller for the Sureños, an American street gang. He was a tattooed, muscular guy called Porky. I never learned his real name. In prison he was "that guy." When he sat down in front of the television, people handed him the remote. When he spoke, everyone got quiet. One day he let me know he was having trouble with the Mexicans. I told him to calm down and not do anything wild.

But he wasn't having it. A few hours later he let me know it was about to "pop off." Before I knew what was happening, horns were blaring and furniture was flying into walls. Two guys beat each other half to death right in front of me. I managed to back away before things got too bad, but not everyone was so lucky. Porky, for instance, found the guy he'd had a problem with and punched him in the head. Then he got hit back *way* harder. By the time everyone was on the ground and the guards were leading guys out in cuffs, Porky was missing half his face. Blood was everywhere. From my cell I watched him get led away, and I thought of something he'd told me the first time I met him.

"I'm a warrior," he'd said, "and I'm serving a life sentence. I'm never going to get out of here, no matter what. And when you're a warrior in here for life, all you have is the people who remember you. Sometimes you have to remind people who you are."

In a strange way, it broke my heart. Here was a guy who'd never see his friends or family again. He'd probably spend the rest of his life in solitary confinement. And the only thing that brought him any comfort in the world was knowing that somewhere, people might be talking about him and how tough he was.

It didn't seem like a good way to live.

Of course, I wasn't exactly the model of clear thinking either. Certainly not during my first days at Santa Ana. One afternoon I learned that a young guy wanted to start a fight with me, so I followed him into his cell, grabbed him, and headbutted him with all my might. Once again I felt a hurricane brewing inside my skull. The pain was almost unbearable. But he'd gotten it much worse. Once he got up from the floor, we talked, and he promised never to bother me again.

Then I tried to go find some Advil.

There were a few other fights, none of which were particularly memorable. After so many years of being the only one in a room willing to throw down at a moment's notice, I was around thousands of guys who were looking for a fight all the time. It was exhausting. All I wanted to do was hang out, talk to people, and pass the time in peace. But getting into altercations was part of prison life. Today they all blend together in my memory—flying fists and concealed shanks and mean-looking gangbangers yelling strange words at me. Somehow, after decades, I'd ended up back in the yard, dodging punches to the head to stay alive.

I hated every second of it.

One morning a guy came up to me after breakfast. He said he was looking for a guy named Bishop.

"That's me," I said.

He looked thrilled.

"I knew it!" he said. "Years ago my girlfriend and I were watching TV, and we saw you and your wife."

I didn't remember the interview, but I believed him. Michelle and I used to be on TV a lot when we were running Living Hope.

"Anyway, my name is Christian," he said. "My girlfriend is now my fiancée, and she's waiting for me on the outside. But she says I need to get my shit together. Find God and all that. So I'm wondering . . ."

"What do you do?"

"Yeah."

I told him the first thing he needed to do was get *The Purpose Driven Life* by Pastor Rick Warren. In the middle of my sentence, he stopped me and walked over to the phones, motioning for me to follow. Before I knew it, I was talking to his fiancée, and she was having me spell out the title so she could order the book and have it shipped to Christian. She ordered a copy for herself too.

Just before Christian hung up, I heard her tell me to look after her fiancé.

It was a task I decided to take seriously.

In the months that followed, Christian and I got close. I learned that he was a fighter like me, only at a much higher level. Over the years he'd competed in many professional MMA fights. In other words, he was exactly the guy you want on your side in prison.

Whenever Christian asked me what books he should have his fiancée send him next, I'd give him my favorites. As time went on, I started dipping back into many of them myself, rediscovering messages that had slipped out of my mind long before. It felt good to be focused on living a good life rather than just surviving again.

A few weeks into this arrangement, Christian came up to me

with a Bible in his hand, confessing that he didn't know where to start. He asked if I could lead a Bible study group, just the two of us.

That same day we sat down across from one another at a table. He asked where I wanted to start.

"In the beginning," I said.

"Like, page one?"

I laughed. "No, man. That's the *line*. Page one. Genesis. 'In the beginning God created the heavens and the earth.'"

He told me to keep going, and I did. The Spirit of God brooding over the primordial waters; Adam and Eve; Cain and Abel.

All of it.

By December 2018 Christian and I had worked our way through a good chunk of the Old Testament, skipping ahead occasionally to study some of the key teachings of Jesus. During that time I noticed he had an aptitude for pulling messages out of the book and phrasing them in ways that everyone around us could understand.

Over time we'd picked up a couple dozen guys. Every day, we'd sit around in a circle, crack our Bibles, and talk. It reminded me of those early days in Vancouver, when I used to sit with the youth group at Neal Curtiss's church, shooting the shit about our lives and talking about how our problems could be solved with God's Word.

It was amazing to watch these tough guys break down in the presence of the Lord. There were days when I completely forgot we were in prison. I'm sure they did too.

Over time, I began ceding the floor to Christian more often. When he spoke, people listened. I got the feeling that he was doing for these guys what I had done for all those people back in

Vancouver when I was young—giving them the Word of God in a way they could relate to, easing their paths into the light of Christ.

For the first time in years, I began feeling like I was doing the right thing.

As the holidays approached, some of the guys in the Bible study began planning a feast to go along with our Christmas Day meeting. We'd stockpile food from the commissary and lay it out on a table. I'd preach, and we'd all eat together, trying to forget that we were locked up. Even the guards seemed okay with it.

Until I ruined the whole thing.

The trouble had started a few weeks earlier, when I started talking with a few guys who didn't speak very good English. They let me know that the prison library didn't have any Bibles in Spanish. So, wanting to help, I started writing letters to the local chapter of the American Civil Liberties Union, trying to see if there was anything they could do to address the issue.

It was probably a stupid thing to do, given how little the prison employees liked people rocking the boat.

But I was in prison, and I had a lot of time on my hands. Also, that pastor's instinct to help people doesn't go away just because you get locked up. If anything, it gets stronger.

What I didn't know at the time was that the prison guards read your mail. *Every* piece of it.

They let me get away with writing a letter a week for a while without saying anything. Then, one morning, I got in line for medicine to help me with a toothache. All I could get, by order of the prison physician, was a single Motrin a day. I'd been finding that the pill, which was supposed to last twelve hours, was wearing off after about six. So I tried to hide it in my cheek when they checked to make sure I'd swallowed it.

And I got caught.

"Are you kidding me?" said the guard. "You're cheeking your meds, and you don't even know how to do it? Aren't you a pastor?"

From then on, I was on notice. The captain called me into her office to sit me down for a heart-to-heart.

"Inmate Bishop," she said, "I have read your file, and to some extent I understand your background as a pastor, which in essence is helping others. I am here to help you understand something. You are in federal prison. You came here alone, and you will one day walk out of here alone. In the meantime, I want you to hear these words, Bishop: Stay in your lane. Stop trying to help everyone. In prison, you can't save the world, and it begins right here and right now."

I nodded in agreement.

As punishment for the Motrin infraction, they put me in solitary confinement for ten days. The sentence, which was handed down on December 18, 2018, meant that I'd be alone in my cell during the Christmas meal that Christian and I had planned for the guys. It also meant I wouldn't be able to speak.

In the days leading up to the meal, Christian came up to my cell door. He said he was thinking about canceling the whole thing. But he couldn't because we'd already spent a few hundred dollars purchasing food for everyone. I'd asked for some leniency from the guards, but they'd told me it wasn't going to happen.

"Here's what you're going to do," I said. "Talk the way you talk during Bible study. Talk about Jesus being born."

"I can't," he said.

"If you are available, I promise you, God will not let you down, my brother. He will speak through you, and when it's over, you will feel and know your words matter to all these men. You don't need me. I'm sorry I let you down. But when we started this Bible study, God knew this moment would be *your moment*. God has you and He knew this would all happen. Be bold. Be graceful. And be *you*."

It was the first time in years that I'd been able to connect with someone so naturally. I was beginning to feel the Holy Spirit moving through me again.

A few days later, on Christmas Day, I watched through a tiny window in my cell as Christian stood up in front of the guys and spoke. He'd slipped some written material under my cell door a day earlier, and I'd taken a look at it. His writing had nearly brought me to tears. And it was bringing other guys to tears too. Over a dinner of commissary chicken and ramen noodles, Christian led the guys in prayer, and I felt proud to know him.

When I was finally released from my "prison within prison" discipline on December 28, we resumed our daily Bible study.

But Christian was leading it now.

Chapter 30

"Wake up," said a voice.

It was no more than three inches from my face. I smelled rotten breath as soon as it spoke.

When I opened my eyes, I saw a face staring back at me. It was covered in more tattoos than I'd ever seen. As I looked at it, the past few days came back to me. I was no longer in Santa Ana. I'd taken a long Con Air flight from there to here, the Oklahoma City Federal Transfer Center. This guy in front of me was one of the many convicts who'd been on the flight with me. I asked what he wanted.

"I need to talk to you," he said, backing up. All the while, he kept his eyes fixed on mine. "I am Jesus Christ, savior of the world. And the world is going to end in ten days."

He held out his wrists, where deep scars peeked out through more tattoos.

I was thoroughly creeped out. So was Joshua, the only guy in the cell other than me and Jesus Christ, savior of the world.

"Yikes," I told him.

"Fifteen days, and the world is going to end. My name is Jesus, and I will save you."

Didn't he just say ten? I thought.

But I only nodded and thanked him for telling me.

In prison it was common to come across crazy people. The best thing to do was sit back, let them rant, and stay on guard. Here at the transfer center, which temporarily housed the guys who had problems at other prisons, the crazy-to-normal ratio was a little skewed. One guy I was being transferred with had been beaten up so badly by inmates at Leavenworth that the feds finally agreed to send him somewhere else. Another had scalded his own back with hot water. For the most part, I got along well with these guys. The only one I couldn't quite reach was the guy who told me he was Jesus every few minutes.

In general, the transfer center wasn't much different from some of the other prisons I'd been to. In the thirty days I was housed there, I talked to guys from all over the country. Many of them asked me about God. I noticed that they all asked the same question about giving their lives over to Christ: "Do I need to do anything?"

To which I'd always say the same thing: "Nothing, brother. You just need to believe that Jesus Christ was who He said He was. He is God, He came down fully human and fully God, and all we have to do is accept and receive His gift of salvation."

That usually made people feel pretty good.

Every time I led someone to Christ, I felt myself getting closer to my true calling again, shedding the past the way a snake sheds its skin. When I called Michelle—which I tried to do every day, though it wasn't always possible—she said I sounded better than I had in years.

But there was also extreme darkness. It was prison, after all. One morning, walking past the cells while the guards were busy, I saw something I'll never forget. A young, skinny Black kid, his eyes devoid of all life, sitting on a bed in a cell. And a line of guys with their heads down, waiting their turn.

Which is probably enough about that.

After a few years in prison, I'd managed to learn the rules. Most of these were small things that you can't find out until you violate them.

For instance, you should never ask another inmate what he's in for. Although it seems like the most natural question in the world, it tends to raise suspicion that you're working for the feds or the courts, wearing a wire to try to get a confession out of someone. I also learned to manage my phone time, which was extremely limited. Every inmate got three hundred minutes a month, limited to fifteen minutes per call. At my first prison, I used it all on calls to Lance and Michelle, and phone minutes were gone in about a week. I spent the rest of that month in the dark about what my friends and loved ones were up to.

The food was usually pretty good. We had hamburgers and french fries on Wednesdays, chicken on the bone on Thursdays, and fish on Fridays. Depending on who was cooking, you could almost forget you were eating prison food.

But in the end, it was still prison. And it sucked.

By the time I was told to "roll it up" at the transfer center so I could move on to my final prison in Florence, Colorado, I could go through all the steps with my eyes closed. I walked out to a van at the right pace, held my shackled hands out for the guard to unlock at the right moment, and stepped in all the right lines at the right times. Other than the Motrin thing, my record was spotless. I was a model prisoner.

But because the prosecutor had painted me in such unflattering terms (flight risk, drug kingpin, demented sociopath), I still had to stay in a maximum-security environment. The prison complex in Florence was enormous, more a small city than a group of prisons. People called it the Alcatraz of the Rockies. At the time I arrived, the surviving Boston Marathon bomber was housed there, along with some of the people alleged to have planned the terror attacks of September 11. I never met any of them, but I did come across some mean dudes.

One of the first things I did was meet with a guy in the laundry room who fitted me for a shirt, pants, and a jacket, the latter item being necessary in Colorado in the dead of winter. Slowly I got the hang of prison economics. Guys traded packets of tuna rather than dollars. We could pass them back and forth in the yard, slipping them into the deep pockets of our jackets, without the guards caring much. Anyone who had a little money in their commissary account—which, thanks to friends and family, I did—could buy things and sell them for a little more than they were worth. Doling out packets of crackers, packets of candy, and cold sodas helped me survive for a while.

Getting contraband wasn't hard. We had something called "the train." Guys who lived nearby would have their families sneak things in using giant duffel bags the size of human beings. You could order items and get them delivered the next week, as long as you paid for them somehow. The bags would be loaded up with food, electronics, and protein powder, then snuck into the prison through friendly guards. Almost half of the guys inside got cell phones this way. But I never did. Michelle told me in no uncertain terms that if I got a cell phone—which was a violation of prison rules and would get me another six months added on to my sentence—she was done with me.

No matter where I went, I'd come across guys who wanted a piece of me. Unlike the cartel dudes, who saw me mostly as a fish out of water who told fun stories, some men in prison saw me as someone they could mess with. I got in a few scraps, but nothing to rival the knock-down, drag-out barfights I'd had in Mexico. Once I dealt with a few aggressors, the normal people tended to leave me alone.

But in prison, not everyone was normal. Some guys just wanted to brawl.

Luckily, God was watching out for me, sending angels to guide me along my path. One of them was a former DEA agent named

Damacio Diaz. Over time, Diaz and I talked about our lives and got around to admitting to our crimes. When I told him what I'd done, he laughed and said he'd seen it a million times before. I learned that he'd gotten mixed up with the cartel, too, and he'd refused to cooperate with the government when he'd been caught. Like me, he was serving a five-year bid. But unlike me, he was a former law enforcement officer. That didn't exactly make him the most popular guy in prison.

During his first few years in Colorado, Diaz got jumped in the shower. He had a guy plant a pack of cigarettes under his pillow to try to get him in trouble. But because he was a nice guy who knew how to talk to the guards, he managed to avoid consequences. By the time I met him in 2019, he was leading the education department for prisoners, trying to help people learn skills that they could use once they got back in the real world. He had a knack for looking at someone, identifying what was holding them back, and working with them to fix it.

I know because he did it with me.

During one of the first conversations we had, Diaz paused and looked me straight in the eye.

"I hear you're a guy who likes to fight," he said.

I told him I was. As he listened, I ran through the problems with anger I'd had my whole life. I told him about the kiddie fight clubs in my uncle's backyard, the scraps with other kids around my neighborhood. I found myself articulating things that I've never been able to say quite the same way since.

When I was done, Diaz asked me why I still got in so many fights.

"I don't know," I told him. "In here, you have to. You can't back down. At some of the places I've been housed at, getting in fights is as normal as taking a shower."

"Doesn't have to be, brother," he said. "In here, there is always someone ready to fight. *Always.* And there is always someone who is stronger and tougher, and it never ends well for you, or for anyone. Even if you win."

I thought about it.

All my life I'd been fighting. Most of the time I'd won. But compared to some of the guys Diaz had known throughout his career, I was nothing. During his time undercover, he'd seen cartel members rip each other apart with their bare hands. He'd seen men driven out to the middle of nowhere, tied to wooden poles, and burned alive. He knew that violence always leads to more violence and that men who live by the sword—or, in my case, the fist, the foot, and the occasional headbutt—would eventually die the same way.

A few weeks later he and I were sitting in the prison chapel watching a movie. Someone demanded we change the channel, and I mouthed off to him, just like I'd done dozens of times before. Before I knew it, the guy—his name was Mike—was standing over me, fists clenched, nostrils flared, daring me to get up and start beating on him. For the first time in my life, I put a little thought into it. I recognized the impulse to get up and brawl for what it was and paused. Then I looked over at Diaz, who said nothing. He didn't have to.

A sense of relief washed over me. I didn't feel like I had anything to prove. When I looked into Mike's angry eyes, I saw the same sense of confusion and rage that had been driving me for more than five decades. And I felt sorry for him. I felt sorry for myself, too, for how many times I'd refused to just do the sensible thing and slow down.

Over the years, during lessons I'd given about the life of Jesus, many people had asked me why He didn't just fight back against the Romans who were persecuting Him. The men crucifying Him asked Him the same thing as He hung on the cross. But I never internalized the lesson that Jesus taught us by remaining gentle and calm in the face of such abuse.

Forgiveness—the thing Jesus was able to do even as He hung from His cross—is the most holy thing a human being can do.

That day in the chapel, I turned down a fight for the first time in my life. And it felt great. In that moment I felt God begin to heal my heart. I knew He had worked through Diaz to keep me calm and help me give up the stupid habit of beating on people that had been forced into me as a kid by irresponsible adults. The path to forgiveness was still foggy, but it was opening up. I was beginning to heal.

In Colorado I entered a drug treatment program that lasted nine months. It was called RDAP. Every three months I'd get a lanyard with a different color, tracing my steps through the process of giving up drugs and alcohol. I began keeping a journal of my time spent in recovery. I talked with guys who were *way* worse off than I'd ever been about how Jesus could help them through their problems, and they listened with rapt attention. I felt myself settling into a routine that wasn't bad.

Near the end of my time in the program, the class voted me a mentor, which brought tears to my eyes for the first time in prison since I'd cried in Miss Ricky's barber chair. I taught classes on ancient Rome and Greece through the prison's education program, a job Diaz had hooked me up with. I led two different Bible studies, one of which met in my cell and grew to twelve guys, the maximum who could pile into my cell with their Bibles before the 9:00 p.m. count. We all used the same devotionals and took turns praying for one another.

Two good friends I made during the Bible studies were Newbie and Dutch, the two shot callers on the block. Both of these men were doing life, and they impressed on me the need to stay calm and do my time so I could get out and see my wife. When the guards left, we took an Amazon Fire TV Stick that someone had snuck into the prison and watched movies in the prison TV room. I made sure they were all Christian movies, and when they were done, I would do a little preaching for the guys. They liked it, and so did I. Joshua, an inmate I'd grown close with, let me know that he thought I might have a future in public speaking.

Michelle visited me once, shortly after working a long summer driving for Uber. She did the fourteen-hour drive with her mother. Seeing her made me want to cry. To this day I get tears in my eyes thinking about the love that came over me when I saw her sitting in the visiting room. In there, the time until my release seemed short. I thought back on all the things in my life that had taken four years. In hindsight, they seemed like nothing.

But back in my cell, those four years seemed like an eternity.

I got through it by repeating a mantra I'd learned in my recovery group. Every day, the group would stand up and recite it.

"Yesterday is history, tomorrow is a mystery, so be your best today."

It was corny in hindsight. But in prison even corny things are worth repeating if they get you through the day.

I decided to take things one day at a time until I could finally get out.

Then my life took a turn.

Chapter 31

From the second I arrived at the Florence prison complex in Colorado, I'd been lightheaded and dizzy.

When I asked the prison doctor about it, he said it was probably vertigo.

"Common problem up here," he said. "You don't know it, but you're at six thousand feet. That'll screw with your system if you're not used to it. It'll go away soon."

But it didn't go away.

One Saturday morning I collapsed in the shower. Two guys had to help me up and get me to the doctor.

Finally he agreed to send me out for an MRI. The prison didn't have a machine, so I climbed in a car with a guard and drove a few miles to the nearest hospital. There was another inmate with us who was getting the same procedure. We didn't talk much. At the hospital they put me on a slab and did the test. I tried asking the MRI tech what was going on, but he wouldn't talk to me. I could tell in his eyes that something wasn't right.

As I put my clothes back on, he said, "You should talk to a doctor."

"I thought you were a doctor," I told him.

"Not me," he said. "We'll have an update for you soon."

Months passed. The vertigo got worse. I started getting bad headaches.

Finally, in October 2019, I got called into the prison doctor's office, where a woman I'd never seen before was sitting at a desk. I took a seat opposite her, detecting something off in her face.

She told me I had a brain tumor.

I froze.

"As you can see here," she said, taking out some charts, "it's what's called a pituitary macroadenoma."

Through the haze of panic in my head, I remembered what little Greek I'd learned at seminary.

"Macro," I said, voice trembling. "That's the big one, right? Like, not *micro*?"

She nodded.

"It's actually . . . well, it's *very* big. I'm going to schedule you for further evaluation in Colorado Springs. It's more than likely that we'll need to do surgery to remove the tumor."

There were other details, but I didn't absorb them in the moment. I was busy wondering whether I'd ever see my wife again, or what she'd do when I died. Even during the years when I lived under the threat of death almost every day, I'd never seriously contemplated the idea that I would soon be gone from this earth. Now death was staring me in the face, burrowing deeper into my brain with each passing second. The tumor was growing, trying to devour me.

As I pored over the charts later, I learned a few things that didn't make me feel any better. The tumor was pressing on my pituitary gland, for instance, and it was dangerously close to my optic nerve. If it continued to grow along its current trajectory, there was a serious possibility that I would wake up one day and be totally blind. The tumor's location also made it so that it could only be accessed surgically through my eye or my nose. The thought of something going into either one of those orifices seriously creeped me out.

By then I had heard horror stories about inmates dying in federal prison. Even on the outside, medical care could be difficult to obtain. In prison it was worse. We weren't exactly the people society wanted to look after, which was why we were locked up in the first place. I was terrified that this surgery would be pushed back so far that I wouldn't have any hope of being saved.

During the weeks between my diagnosis and my surgery, I repeated a verse I had studied for years, admiring its simplicity and power.

"Don't worry about anything; instead, pray about everything" (Philippians 4:6 NLT).

Of course, when you have a brain tumor, that's much easier said than done.

A year after my initial diagnosis, I finally went in for surgery.

In that time COVID-19 swept through the prison and killed a few dozen inmates. We were all in close quarters, and we had no idea how contagious or lethal the virus would be. I managed to escape it, but the relief wasn't as sweet given the foreign body eating up my brain tissue.

I'd also met a doctor in prison who helped me understand what I was going through. He'd sit with me after Bible study was over and answer any questions. He never told me what he was in for, and I never asked. But I'm grateful for the kindness he showed me.

The actual process for getting the surgery was complicated. Given the COVID protocols, guards weren't allowed to touch prisoners or get too close to them. So when the guard came into my cell at three thirty in the morning to wake me up, he had to kick my bed until I stirred. I jolted upright, not knowing what was going on. I later learned that the surgery times were kept a secret so that prisoners couldn't plan an escape.

I wanted to call Michelle. Over the past year she'd been the one thing that distracted me from worrying. But I wasn't given the option to use a phone. I just walked, still bleary-eyed from sleep, and got in the back of a van.

We arrived at the hospital around six o'clock in the morning, and the corrections officer checked me in. I heard someone mention that the name of this place was Memorial Hospital—the same name as the place in Vancouver where I'd been taken after getting my nose kicked in so many years earlier.

A few minutes later I was sitting up in a bed in a gown, and someone was explaining exactly what they were going to do to me. I could barely listen. I was so nervous. But I found the strength to pray for all the medical professionals who were going to handle my surgery, knowing there was a very real possibility that I wouldn't make it.

The next thing I knew, the mask was over my face, and I was slipping into blackness.

I managed to open my eyes a few hours after the surgery.

But I could tell something was wrong.

Doctors were all over the room, which didn't look anything like the one I'd been in before the surgery. Machines beeped. Tubes jutted out from my body in all directions. The first doctor came in, reading from a clipboard and preparing to tell me what was wrong. His name was Dr. Capen.

"See all those people out there?" he said.

I looked to my left and saw a crowd of doctors behind glass.

"Yes," I said, my voice hoarse.

"We're all working to figure out what's wrong with you. At the moment, your kidneys are emptying all the blood sodium from your body. Normally we want your levels between 137 and 143. Yours are below 100. I don't want to alarm you, but we are thinking about removing your skull cap. With the lack of sodium, your brain is swelling in a way we cannot control or manage."

I asked if that meant what I thought it meant.

He said yes.

Doctors were considering sawing the top of my head off to ease the swelling in my brain. As the guy spoke, I couldn't help but think of how poorly I'd treated my head over the years. Visions of hard punches to the skull and the headbutt I'd delivered to that guy in prison flooded my swelling brain. I felt like I was half in a dream and half out of it, only I couldn't seem to wake up.

Hours later a kidney specialist entered the room.

He looked sullen.

After running through a few test results and throwing some numbers at me that I didn't understand, he asked if he could be honest with me.

I said yes.

"You are more than likely going to die."

I panicked, but I tried not to let anything show on my face.

"I will be back to talk with you in a couple of hours, and I will look into any and all options. But it appears we have exhausted all viable, life-sustaining treatments. If you want us to call a priest for last rites, we can do that. Otherwise, I'll be back soon."

Memories flashed through my head. The doctor back in Vancouver who'd said *If you have a priest, I'd call him now.* Neal Curtiss praying at my bedside, thinking I'd slip away at any moment. I thought of Chucho, whose funeral I'd performed just a few years ago. I thought of Michelle, David, Katie, Hannah, and my grandkids, wondering how they'd survive without me. I wanted to call someone. But I could barely move.

I'd never felt so alone in my life.

When the doctor left the room, I felt the same sense of abandonment I'd been feeling all my life, ever since my dad died when

I was four years old. The pain was intense. An emptiness formed inside me and grew for the next hour, which felt like an eternity.

When the kidney specialist came back in, I figured he was going to stick a mirror under my nose and check for fog marks.

But he surprised me by offering a last-ditch option to save me.

"We've got a Hail Mary," he said. "It's unlikely to work, but in your case, I think it's worth a shot."

He was talking about a drug called tolvaptan, which hadn't yet been approved by the FDA. The side effects could be brutal, but as far as I could tell, none of them was worse than dying.

I agreed.

Not being Catholic, I've never said a Hail Mary prayer in my life. I didn't even know all the words.

But I said other prayers, most of which were delivered to God in the same honest, free-flowing style I'd always used to preach.

I asked for a miracle. I asked Him to look after my children and my wife. I asked forgiveness for all the people I had hurt and wronged in my life.

For a few hours I heard nothing back.

The machines beeped. Footsteps echoed in the ICU hallway. A guard sat in a chair in the corner of my room reading a magazine, refusing to talk to me or make eye contact.

I was at the end of myself.

The moment Elijah had reached in the wilderness.

And I was alone.

I thought of the verse from the Gospel of John, in which Jesus finds out that Lazarus has died.

"Jesus wept," it says (11:35).

It's the shortest verse in the whole Bible.

Lying there in my bed, feeling the effects of the drug beginning to work on my system, I tried to weep. But I had no tears. I was about to die in a small room with no one but a mute security guard to comfort me. I didn't even want the priest they'd offered to send me. I wanted my wife and my children. I wanted to live.

By then almost everyone I'd known in Mexico was dead. I was sure of it. And I was about to join them.

Just then a voice—as in a real voice, as human as anything I'd ever heard in my life—spoke to me.

I am here, I heard. *I love you and I will never leave or forsake you. You are My son, and I love you so much.*

I looked around the room.

No one was in it but me and the guard.

You will not die here.

I managed to sit up and ask the guard whether he'd heard anything.

He said no, then looked right back down at his magazine.

"I just heard God speak to me," I told him. "That was God."

He looked up.

"Probably the drugs," he said. "But good for you."

I'd heard the voice of God before. He'd told me to climb in the water during one of my first church services. He'd led me to make just about every decision I'd ever made as the founder of Living Hope. But I'd never heard His voice as clearly as I did sitting up in that hospital bed, contemplating my own death.

And the message—*I will never leave or forsake you*—was exactly the one I needed to hear.

All my life I'd lived with a crippling fear that everyone was going to leave me. That's why I'd always sought to give people more stuff, to keep talking long past the point when we all should have gone to bed. I tried to buy the affection of people, including members of my own family. I believed that if I was entertaining enough to my friends, it would keep them from abandoning me the way my father and stepfather had.

And here was my heavenly Father, telling me He would never abandon me.

That might sound simple to some people, especially if you've never dealt with abandonment. But for me, it was perfect.

I leaned my head back on the pillow, knowing I was going to live.

My story wasn't over yet.

Part 5

ALMOST HOME

Chapter 32

Early in my prison term I got an email from an old friend, Ron Webb.

As soon as I saw his name on the grainy screen of the prison computer, my mind flashed back to all the memories I had of him. I saw him banging his fists on the table during our first meeting, then pulling me aside to admit that God had spoken to his heart and changed his mind.

He wanted to know how I was.

I wrote back, letting him know that I'd been better.

But we kept up a correspondence that lasted the entire length of my incarceration. At four different prisons I emailed Ron to let him know I was still hanging in there. He helped me through my brain tumor, my surgery, and the months of recovery that followed. When I was let out of prison on early release in 2021, largely thanks to my efforts at drug recovery, he was among the first people to congratulate me. He said that one day, when I was ready, he wanted me to speak at his church in Vancouver, a small place called New Life Friends.

I didn't see myself ever speaking in church again. I wasn't even sure I'd ever *go* to church again. The memories of what had happened to me, and what I had done to other people, were too painful. I spent one month in a halfway house and five months under house arrest after getting out. It wasn't great, but it was much better than prison. I got to see Michelle and my family for a few months at a time. David came to one of these visits and let me know that he'd given up on dealing drugs and hanging with cartel guys for good, though he still wouldn't come home from Mexico. He and his wife, Arisbeth, had a son and named him John. Michelle and I still had our single-wide trailer in Yuma, Arizona, not much bigger than the first house we'd ever bought as a married couple. But it felt like our home.

I spent a long time wondering what I was going to do. I figured I could always start another diesel repair business with David, who'd had his own business the whole time I was in prison. I applied for a greeter job at Walmart, but they rejected me.

Life isn't easy for a felon.

Especially not one whose story had been written about in dozens of major newspapers, including a full feature story in *Vanity Fair*.

The one thing I was sure I'd never do was set foot in Vancouver, Washington, again. There were too many people who knew my story. There I figured people would scream at me in the streets. I imagined horrible scenes of embarrassment every time I tried to stop at Denny's for a burger or go to Costco for groceries. There was no way people wouldn't know who I was.

So I tried a few different things. My mother helped me and my family by providing some money despite her fixed income. Our friends stepped in and gave money when they could. The film rights to my story ended up being acquired by a production company, which helped. But the purpose in my life was gone. I didn't know what to do. Over the years, I had ministered to many people who found themselves in similar circumstances. I had noticed that people who were lost tended to fall back on what they knew. In the Bible we have many verses that depict the disciples falling back on fishing, which was how they passed the time before Jesus restored their lives.

But I had never been a fisherman.

I'd known only business and ministry for most of my life.

And drinking. Although I had managed to keep that demon at bay for most of my life—pretty much from the day I married Michelle until things started to go sideways for me at Living Hope—the urge to hit the bottle never really went away. Whenever I had serious problems in my life (and I had a *lot* of serious problems, as you've seen), I felt the pull of liquor as strongly as I'd felt it as a confused kid. Even in prison I managed to get my hands on hard liquor on occasion, and the sweet burn of it momentarily took away my troubles.

I'd kept up drinking when I got out of prison, much to my shame. Sometimes I hid it from Michelle, and sometimes I didn't. She was worried for me, but there wasn't much I could do to stop myself. One afternoon in 2023 we began a road trip up to Portland, Oregon, for a family reunion, and I stopped at the VA hospital there to get my tumor checked on. Before the hospital, though, we took an old friend up on an offer to tour the current Living Hope building, which still houses the church with most of our old friends. As soon as I walked in, I saw Kevin, the guy who'd saved all my DVDs and files from the dumpster, standing with a camera. We embraced, though Michelle was a little nervous to be filmed. Walking around the old building, I felt numb. I walked across the floor, running my hand over the seats. On each one, there was a name scrawled in black Sharpie. Years earlier, during a message, I had instructed everyone in the building to write the name of someone who wasn't there—someone who needed to find God, who needed a second chance—on the backs of their chairs. Most people had done it. With my head pounding and my body aching, I sat in one of the chairs and looked up at the stage where I had preached so many messages. Michelle stood beside me.

"I just don't get it," I said. "All these people, and . . . I mean, why wasn't I worth a second chance?"

Just being in the building hurt like hell. We walked outside, back to the car, and headed for the hospital. There the doctors took one look at me and said I needed to go to rehab immediately. I vividly remember one of them saying, "If you keep doing this to your body, you're going to die."

I knew they were right.

Lance and Carolyn drove me to Legacy Hospital in Vancouver, Washington. Over the next few days, I detoxed from the booze and tried to get my head on straight, fully aware that I was lying in bed less than a mile from Manor Grange, where we'd started Living Hope. Somehow I had ended up in the last place on earth I wanted to be, doing the last thing on earth I wanted to do. I thought of all the sermons I'd given over the years encouraging people to do the hard thing in their lives—to examine the darkest corner of themselves and have the strength to deal with whatever they found there. *Reveal what you feel, and you'll begin to heal* was how I'd always put it during my days as a pastor to thousands of people. And yet, even during my time in federal prison, I had never taken my own advice.

The detoxing was rough, but I got through it. On the first night of my stay, a nurse brought me shepherd's pie, which had always been my favorite meal. The taste of it instantly reminded me of the story of Elijah. Just like him, I was still running away from what I needed to do. And just like him, I felt like I was getting nourishment straight from God. I don't know why that detail sticks out in my memory, but it does.

Before I knew it, I was in the car with Michelle outside the hospital, staring down at my phone. A text had just come in from someone I felt like I had known in another life, before the downfall and the cartel and the guns and all the horrible mistakes I had made.

"I have something I want you to do," said Ron Webb.

I asked what he was talking about.

"Just come meet my pastor," he said. "Have lunch."

I thought about it for a second. But I was always going to say yes. For one thing, I truly believe God was pushing me in that direction. Also, I have never in my life turned down a free lunch, and I wasn't about to start.

Officially, Ron's church was called New Life Friends. But everyone in town knew it as "The Lord's Gym." On the side of the building, there was a giant mural of Jesus Christ, looking out on the surrounding neighborhood with all its vacant storefronts and run-down houses. The building itself was an old pizza parlor called Uncle Milt's. Given its location in a rough, crime-ridden part of Vancouver, the building's small parking lot was surrounded by a chain-link fence that included a gate and locks. The congregation, I knew, wasn't big. They almost never broke thirty people in a Sunday service.

During lunch Pastor Dave White asked me to speak at a service that weekend. When I asked him what I would talk about, he looked at me like I was nuts. He said, "I don't know. I mean, whatever you want." Lance, who'd also come along to lunch, seemed to agree.

I guess I understood his confusion. In all my years working as a pastor, I'd never had a hard time coming up with things to say. Back in the heyday of Living Hope, you could have told me to do twenty minutes on the importance of sugar packets, and I probably could have done it, then wrapped it up by quoting a few choice verses from the New Testament.

But there was an elephant in the room now.

Although it wasn't Living Hope, Ron's church was still smack-dab in the middle of Vancouver, Washington. I would have bet all the money in my bank account—which wasn't much at the time—that every single person who'd show up to Sunday's service would have heard my story. It had run almost every day in the local newspaper, after all. A reporter had shown up to court every day and penned a six-part investigative series that made it seem like I was a cross between Pablo Escobar and Satan. I didn't know how to address it. After lunch, Ron and Pastor White led me around the building. They showed me a large area with folding tables where people came from all over town to have dinner. Almost every night of the week, they said, volunteers came in and cooked food for kids who couldn't get hot meals at home. Lately, families on government assistance had begun coming in to get some food in their stomachs.

I was surprised. For years I had traveled to churches and taken tours just like this one. Even the ones who did the most charitable work usually sat dormant during the week. They offered breakfast on Saturdays, services on Sundays, and nothing until the next weekend. This was different. I felt that Pastor White and his team were serving people just as Jesus had told us to in the Bible. They were serving as the hands of God on earth.

On the main floor, there were treadmills and weight benches that the Portland Trail Blazers had donated years before. I walked around, touching each one, remembering all the hours I'd spent lifting weights as an angry kid. Upstairs, there was a boxing ring and a few piles of gloves. Looking at it, I felt something stir in me.

The same voice that had spoken to me back at the hospital came back, a little quieter this time.

This is where you're supposed to be, it said.

And I knew it was right.

That was how I found myself standing before the congregation in August 2023, dressed in a button-down shirt and khaki pants, stumbling a little on my aching legs. By this point, almost every joint in my body was in pain. I had headaches all the time. The abuse to which I had subjected myself over the years was beginning to show, and I wasn't using booze to numb the pain anymore. But as soon as I began speaking, the pain went away. So did all the noise in my head. I felt like I was home.

I confessed my transgressions to a crowd of more than four hundred people, some of whom I knew, most of whom I didn't. I repented publicly, and I said I was sorry for hurting so many people who had counted on me to lead them by example. Then I asked the crowd if they could forgive me. They nodded their heads. I cracked a few jokes and made my way through a loose sermon, feeling that I was back on the right track for the first time in years.

Pastor White had offered me a position as the lead pastor at the church a few days earlier, and I had accepted without telling anyone, including Michelle. When she heard me announce that I'd taken the job from the back of the room, she was as surprised as anyone. Before I knew it, we were packing up the car and coming back to Vancouver, the place where we had met, built a church, and lived so many wonderful years of our lives. Over the next few months, my new associates and I got to work.

The fence was the first thing to go. I didn't like the idea of preaching in a church that wanted to keep people out. We made some cosmetic improvements, and we began serving free breakfast and dinner to more people than ever. Today people come from all over town to sit and pray with us in the morning. I was warned that we might get graffiti or other kinds of vandalism if we took down the fence and began letting people in, but as of this writing, it hasn't happened. And I don't expect it to.

The thing I'm the proudest of, which happens every day, is seeing so many people in our community loved, served, and helped, not just on Sundays but every day of the week. These volunteers inspire me to be a better person.

And then there's the boxing ring upstairs. Every day, kids who have anger problems and no fathers to guide them—kids like *me*, in other words—come in, put on gloves, and battle it out with one another for a few minutes. A lot of the time, they'll sit with someone and talk, which is almost as good. People often ask me whether I'm afraid of retribution, given how much I've talked about the Sinaloa Cartel. I tell them that almost every second of every day, I'm surrounded by some of the scariest, meanest—and yet most kindhearted—people in the world. I've hired many people who've just gotten out of prison. Some of them are pastors. Joshua, my closest friend from prison, has been working for us since May 2024, doing wonderful work on the recovery side of our church.

We've told the police around Vancouver that if they ever encounter a kid who's making trouble in the streets, they're more than welcome to drop the kid here at The Lord's Gym. They've taken me up on that offer many times. I'll sit with the kids and talk just like I used to during my first days as a youth pastor, and I'll see if they want to try some more constructive ways of getting out their aggression. No one ever gets hurt. No one takes hard hits to the head the way I did as a kid.

Sometimes people ask me if I miss preaching to thousands of people every Sunday, and I say no every time. I've done the megachurch thing. Although I never had much money, I enjoyed being able to reach so many people at once. But if there's one thing I've learned over the course of my journey, it's that the work of God gets done in small moments. I don't think it's an accident that everywhere I've gone, from the barrios of Tijuana to the worst prisons in the United States, I've led people to Christ, and I've usually done it by accident. For the first time in a long time, I feel like I'm doing the right thing, allowing God to work through me to spread His Word around the world—or, at least, through my little corner of Vancouver, Washington.

It's not lost on me how lucky I am to be alive. Many of the people you've read about in this book aren't. Memo is dead, and so are two out of the three Victors. My handler, whose name I don't even remember, is dead. I'm sure that many of the people who stood with me over Chucho's coffin in the desert are also buried in unmarked graves somewhere nearby. If spending time around these people has taught me anything, it's that life is precious. Within every person, there is a whole universe. There's pain, joy, and the capacity to love unconditionally. We're all God's children. Every time I meet a kid who's been making trouble around town, lashing out just so he can feel something, I think back on what it was like to be a scared kid without a father, just flailing around looking for something to make me feel alive. I remember that all I needed was someone to pull me aside and tell me that I mattered and that I was enough.

For that reason, I believe that the work I'm doing right now is the most important work I've ever done. A day spent helping one person at a time, telling one person at a time that there is a God who sees them and loves them for who they are, is never wasted. Instead of seeing thousands of people baptized, I'm seeing one person at a time saved. I feel incredibly grateful to still have Michelle by my side and to know that our children (and our children's children) are safe despite all the danger I put them in. If I could drive to the homes of everyone in Vancouver whose feelings I hurt through my actions and apologize, I would do it tomorrow. But that's not going to happen. So I'm going to do the only thing I know how to do: live my life one day at a time, leading as many people into the light of God as I can.

And I'm just getting started.

Acknowledgments

Thank You, God, who knows me best and loves me most. You knew me before I was born. You have allowed every breath in my body, and my story and mess will become *Your* message to a world that needs to know how loved they are, no matter what.

Thank You, Jesus, for being with me when I almost died in Memorial Hospital in Vancouver and then Memorial Hospital thirty years later in Colorado Springs. I love You and give every moment of my life to serving You.

Mama: You are the best mother I could have hoped for. All my years of searching for a father, I missed the most precious person who gave birth to me, who has been there with and for me. Mama, I love you. I wish I could take away all the pain I watched you endure. XOXOXOXO

David: Thank you, son, for always loving me when there were so many days I couldn't love myself. Our road trip was one of the best memories of my entire life. I love you and am so proud of you.

Katie: I love you more than I have words for. You have the most generous heart to forgive others, and your love for Jesus is so abundantly obvious. You are the best wife for Jordan and the best mama to Isaiah, Titus John, Malachi, Ruthie, and little Micah. I love you and could not be more proud.

Hannah-Jo: I love you, baby girl. You are a warrior for Jesus, a great wife, and a mom to Judah (Bear). I see you traveling around, and it reminds me of those precious times when we were in Australia, New Zealand, and so many other places, telling people about Jesus. I love you.

Candise: How can I begin to thank you? A big sister, protector, and one of the most encouraging people I have ever known. You prayed every day for seven years. God answered you and then some. Thank you from the bottom of my heart. Everyone needs a candid Candise.

Brother (Mike): Not sure where to even begin, but you have been there for my family for all the years I couldn't and wasn't. I love you and can never pay you back for all you have done for my family and me.

Dad and Sharon: I never planned on living in Yuma, but I am so glad for the years Michelle lived there and you could be with her. It's so heartwarming to see Dad pull up on his golf cart to visit us. You both have become so close to my heart. Sharon, thanks for reading all my books. I love you both.

Keith and Vicki: Wow. Thank you. I love you both. You stepped in as family to take care of Michelle when I was unable to do so and continued even after I was released from prison. It's beautiful to see a friendship develop into everything love could and should be.

Ron and Marilyn: Thanks for never giving up on me when most of the world did. You are and always will be spiritual parents to me. Your wisdom, encouraging words, and sometimes correction have always helped me strive to be a better person, Jesus follower, and husband.

Lance and Carolyn: You have been best friends, helpful in every measurable way, patient and forgiving, and, simply, I love you both. I'm still not sure how I begged you to move to Yuma, and then God moved me to Vancouver—but we'll be back.

Joshua: Thank you so much. Words can't begin to express the journey that we have begun together—a journey that began in federal prison. And now you have moved halfway across the United

States to be with us and to help us become all that God wants us to be. Michelle and I love you so much, and we count you as family.

Jim Kleiser: You are a good friend, and I love you. I owe you for years of storage and so much more.

Christian Bale: Thank you, my friend. You were the first to believe in this story and in me. I'll never forget the countless hours we spent together. You are one of the most genuine and generous people I have ever met. You were both a friend and a therapist, helping us work through our story. Through it all, you believed in me. I'll never forget your quote: "At least I tried, damn it."

Mark and MJ (who is with Jesus), and Maddie: Thank you for never forgetting me when I was in prison. Your support, friendship, and encouragement have become one of the best parts of my life. More than anything, you reminded me that God was going to use me. I love you, Mark. Madeline, you being a part of what God is doing at New Life has truly given me a sense of new life for ministry. You are so blessed; you are so gifted. It is my honor to be the Elijah in your life. I love your family.

Pastor Dave and Renee White: Thank you for that first lunch and for offering me a second chance. I'm not sure if you'll understand until heaven how much it meant that you believed in me when no one else did. Your faith and dedication to Jesus have had an eternal impact.

Jim LeShana and the entire Friends Denomination: When we first met in Newberg, I didn't know what to expect—and certainly didn't expect to be welcomed, received, and restored by you and others. There's no question that God has bigger plans than we can begin to see. Thank you for letting me join with you.

New Life Church: There are no words that exist in the universe of words. You helped me find a second chance. You have helped when you were tired. Had faith when it didn't make sense. I love each and every one of you. You already know this.

Sean McGowan: Thank you. You are a friend and helped make

this book better than it ever would have been. Your wisdom, kindness, and hundreds of hours will certainly make a difference. I can't imagine doing any writing project without you. You were patient when emotions were high, you laughed at my sometimes stupid jokes, and you gently kept me on track. I love you and hope the best for you and your family always.

Ian Kleinert: You are the best agent, an amazing friend, and you have helped me in more ways than just this project. You guided me through the process with insight and patience. You listened as a brother when I was struggling and advocated for me always. You are simply the best.

My dear friend Eric Robinson: You believed in this project before anyone else did. I will never forget meeting you while I was in prison and emailing back and forth about ideas. I can't believe all we dreamed about is beginning to take shape. Ellen should promote you.

Matt Baugher, my publisher and friend (SVP HarperCollins): Thank you for seeing the potential in my story. I truly appreciate you, and it isn't by coincidence (there's no word for this in the Greek language) that you were Billy Graham's publisher for all those years. What an honor to work with you. I look forward to all that God has for us going forward.

Austin Ross, my editor: Thank you for all the hard work you have done and, I am certain, will continue to put into this book. I look forward to meeting in person someday. Thanks so much.

Ellen Goldstein, President of Gotham Entertainment and Productions: You have been so instrumental in this project from conception to execution and all the details in between. I am excited to meet you in person. Thanks for helping my wife while I was in prison. You remember.

Aboriginal Merchants: Your willingness to allow me to tell my whole story has changed my life and I hope will impact the world in some small way. I hope each of you are blessed for your flexible generosity.

My wife, Michelle, my best friend, the mother of our three amazing children, and the best grandma to our eight grandkids: I dedicate this journey, of course, to God—and to you. Neither of you have left me. I knew God wouldn't; I knew you could have. Your undeniable and contagious faith and your strength in the face of trials and storms have inspired thousands. Your resolve to never quit and to always do what Jesus did is remarkable. You love when it doesn't make sense and forgive when it seems undeserved. I love you with all my heart, and I am sorry for how I have hurt you. I will spend every waking moment of my life proving that we are worth it.

With all my heart,
John

Notes

23 “But there never seems to be enough time”: “Time in a Bottle,” by Jim Croce, produced by Terry Cashman and Tommy West, ABC Records ABC-11405, 45 rpm, released as a single in November 1973.

64 Just over 30 percent of people regularly attended services: Pew Research Center, “Unaffiliated (Religious ‘Nones’),” *Religious Landscape Study*, accessed November 30, 2017, https://web.archive.org/web/20171130131524/http://www.pewforum.org/religious-landscape-study/religious-tradition/unaffiliated-religious-nones/.

79 *Outreach Magazine* ranked us: Lynne Marian, “Outreach Magazine Updates List of Top 100 Largest & Fastest-Growing US Churches,” *Outreach*, October 24, 2007, https://www.outreach.com/articles/mobilefriendlyview?article_name=a-top10007.

89 “I know David has made wrong choices”: John Bishop, *God Distorted: How Your Earthly Father Affects Your Perception of God and Why It Matters* (Multnomah Books, 2013), introduction.

119 “In the lowest deep a lower deep”: John Milton, *Paradise Lost*, ed. John Leonard (Penguin Classics, 2003), book 4, line 76.

About the Author

John Lee Bishop is the senior pastor at New Life Church in Vancouver, Washington, and was the cofounder of Living Hope Church, which he led for twenty years. During his leadership, Living Hope was recognized as the seventh-fastest-growing church in America, with campuses in the Northwest United States, Hawaii, India, and New Zealand. It was also the only church he ever planted, making this achievement particularly significant.

John has spoken at numerous pastor conferences and evangelistic crusades across seventeen countries, including Nicaragua, South Korea, India, Australia, and New Zealand, sharing his passion for faith and leadership worldwide.

He earned a master of arts in evangelism and transformational leadership from Western Seminary in Portland, Oregon, furthering his dedication to inspiring and guiding others in their spiritual journeys.

John and his wife, Michelle, reside in Vancouver, Washington. They have been happily married for forty-one years and are the proud parents of three adult children—David, Katie, and Hannah—and grandparents to eight wonderful grandchildren, with hopes for even more in the future.

Free Bonuses

Access an exclusive video of chapter 1 read by John Lee Bishop, bonus commentary about his experience, and more free gifts and resources.

www.johnleebishop.com/bonus